CONTENTS

King Mob	1
Introduction	3
1 - New York 1967: King Mob and Black Mask	9
2 - King Mob at Selfridges, December 1968	36
3 - The 1970 Situationist Reorientation Debate	40
4 - Nietzsche, Wagner and the Theatricalisation of MusiC	46
5 - Kurt Schwitters' Barn: A Tale of Two Cities	54
6 - Malevich in the 21st Century	66
7 - The Physical Impossibility of Damian Hirst in the Minds of the Living	81
8 - Meccano on Crack (Or Tatlin on Crack)	95
9 - All the Way to the Bank(sy)	108
10 - Mayakovsky and Tatlin	125
11 - Ralph Rumney	151

KING MOB

The Negation and Transcendence of Art

*

David and Stuart Wise

WisEbooks Series No. 3

*

BPC Publishing

*

London

*

**Copyright © 2024
All Rights Reserved**

*

http://thebarbarismofpureculture.co.uk/wp

*

BPC101Radpub@gmail.com

INTRODUCTION

In the mid-1960s, DavidWise (born 1943) and Stuart Wise (1943-2021) were students at Newcastle University School of Art. They were associated with what they later called 'the often confusedly anti-art magazine', *Icteric*. The magazine's purported aim was the 'fusion' of 'art and life'. It was mainly the brainchild of Ronald Hunt, librarian at the Dept of Fine Art at Newcastle University, who had been appointed on the recommendation of lecturer and pop artist, Richard Hamilton. As a librarian Hunt was familiar with the more marginal publications of the international art scene. It was he who first acquainted future English Situationist member Donald Nicholson-Smith with the theoretical journals of the Paris-based Situationist International. Hunt also learned of the activities the *Black Mask* group in New York, such as their intervention at a meeting in a plush art gallery shouting, 'burn the museums baby', 'art is dead', 'Museum closed' etc.

Dave Wise recalls in *King Mob: A Critical Hidden History*:

> 'Soon letters were sent out to New York and we got replies immediately: "brothers/sisters come and join us"! So two of us (Dave Wise and Anne Ryder) went from Newcastle to New York via London, and in the summer of 1967 engaged in some of the activities of Black Mask... Having by then heard of the Situationists in New York, Ben Morea gave us the personal addresses and telephone numbers of Sit sympathisers who resided in London. We duly contacted on them on our return to England. They were the people around the magazine Heatwave, some of whom initially formed the English section of the

Situationist International. Heatwave was the first magazine of all to put the new revolt of youth into some kind of perspective, with specific reference to Mods and Rockers, Beats and the like; affirming their vandalistic acts of destruction as something which could have real future consequences.'

Initially, what resulted was a 'meeting - if you like – between north and south': between the Wise twins and friends, and the English section of the Situationists, consisting of, Chris Gray, Donald Nicholson Smith, Tim (TJ) Clark and Charles Radcliffe. In this new grouping the ideas of the Situationists and their predecessors were discussed in depth,

'...finding out by word of mouth - from the horse's mouth if you like - all the unknown history of post-Second World War cultural and political subversion and how we could no longer separate the two as they inevitably tended more and more to enmesh. Astonished, we heard about the International Lettrist interventions in the 1950s, particularly Michel Mourre's invasion of Notre Dame dressed as a priest incarnating a litany proclaiming "God is Dead" only to be set upon by the Swiss Guards with swords drawn ready to hack him to pieces, finally escaping with some nasty cuts. That all this information been withheld from us only confirmed what we'd felt deep down all our lives: England was a truly conservative shit hole!' At that time a magazine was being put together containing new, original polemical texts, most of which – due to 'unforeseen circumstances - have unfortunately been lost as the proposed magazine never saw the light of day:

'We saved the only known one: The Revolution of Modern Art and the Modern Art of Revolution put together by Chris Gray and Don with occasional help from Tim Clark... In that text there are references to Black Mask couched in a comradely critical way. And then came Vaneigem's bombshell communication after his meeting with Black Mask in New York in late 1967. Principally, Vaneigem objected to Alan Hoffman, a kind of mystical but political acidhead who'd started to show an interest in Black Mask... Also, Ben had a serious liver complaint and he couldn't touch alcohol, thus acid went down very nicely... Ben was inevitably very upset about Vaneigem and started raving on in letters about the man-of-letters disposition Vaneigen put across, accusing him of not knowing anything about those at the bottom of the pile and street life in general. This created quite a dilemma in London as Chris Gray and Don N Smith in particular wanted to keep all the newfound friendships here alive and kicking. Knowing our friendliness with Ben Morea, they didn't want to cause too many upsets before things had really kicked in in terms of doing something together. Presumably because of their prevarication, they were excluded from the Situationists and the rest, as they say, is history... Out of this lacunae and initial disorientation followed by a kind of re-think, King Mob developed.'

'It could be said that King Mob had created an opening out of nothing in these islands and that is something that adds up to la gloire! Aggressive tactics had split something asunder as basically we were absolute beginners without any immediate reference points to hand. It's like as though we were forced into the quasi-terrorist address against a back drop of quite terrifying incomprehension. Hardly surprising therefore that it was followed by direct action terrorism in the form of the Angry Brigade even though both were heading clean up the wall. By 1972, we realised we had nothing to fall back onto. Nobody would possibly publish anything we'd done or would even propose to do so.'

As the texts in this volume will show, the Wise twins and their King Mob friends continued their activism and theoretical outpourings long after the King Mob 'moment', separate from, ignored by, and indeed, despised by former associates who 'survived' by getting careers in journalism, publishing and academia. etc. To physically survive and finance their publications, the ex-King Mobbers formed a builders' collective called the Lascar Apprentices, who were all paid the same wage and were in constant conflict with the hated construction industry contractors.

On the website of *Tate Britain* there is an article by Hari Kunzru, entitled 'The mob who shouldn't really be here: King Mob' (1 May 2008). One suspects that this piece was commissioned by the Tate to 'explain' how some of the productions of the group which opposed institutions like art museums ended up in ... art museums:

'As revolutionary bullshit detectors and anti-art activists, King Mob despised one thing above all – culture, "the commodity which helps sell all the others." To them Godard was "just another bloody Beatle," and the elite of cultural consumers who looked to the avant-garde or the political underground for shock or novelty were just as duped by the spectacle as any mass-media-watching suburbanite. And that means you, readers of Tate Etc. One thing is certain. King Mob never wanted to find themselves here, in the house rag of cultural consumption, let alone locked away in

Tate's permanent collection. But these posters and magazines are just detritus, the record of past struggles. In the present day, the real action is elsewhere.'

Whatever 'real action' consists of, and wherever 'elsewhere' might be, is best left to Kunzru to explain. As for 'detritus' of 'past struggles', perhaps the detritus has more claim to relevance than what is today claimed in the 'art world' (and politics) to be 'substantial' (a dictionary definition of the opposite of detritus is 'substance'); and perhaps past struggles have more to teach us than present-day capitulations to capital.

In this collection of documents written over a 50-year period, the Wises describe their involvement with other influential radicals who set out to subvert the capitalist system and its culture industry. They also reflect on why the Revolution 'due to unforeseen circumstances' did did take place and on the process of recuperation of radical aesthetic ideas was evidenced in the works of latter-day chancers such as Damiam Hurst and Banksy. It is hoped that this book, along with the other two titles published this year (2024) in the BPC/WisEbooks series will, in some small (non-anti-academic) way, challenge the 'official' cultural history regarding King Mob; and, to borrow Edward Thompson's famous phrase in *The Making of the English Working Class*, rescue that history from the 'enormous condescension of posterity'.

David Black

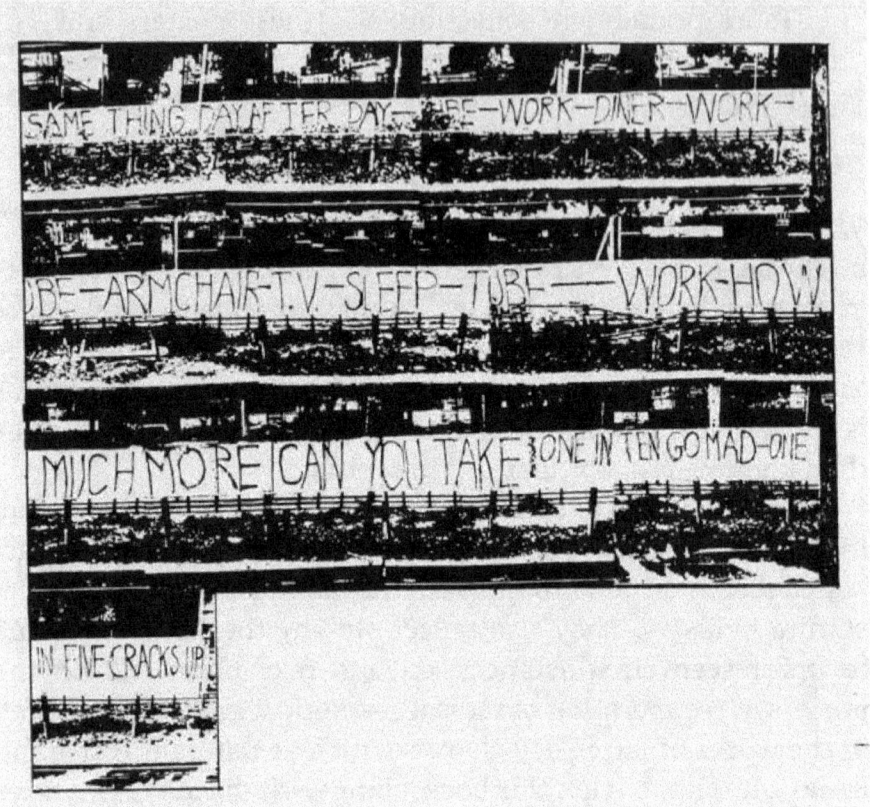

King Mob railway graffiti 1968

1 - NEW YORK 1967: KING MOB AND BLACK MASK

Dave and Stuart Wise
2007

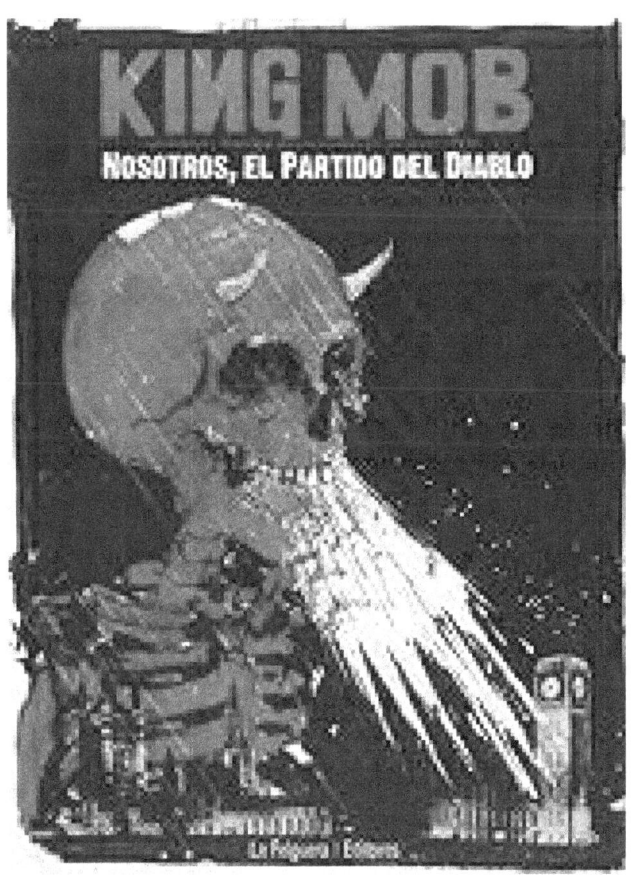

From and introduction for a book in Spanish on Black Mask & The Motherfuckers

King Mob. Nosotros, el Partido del Diablo was published in 2015. It came about as a result of correspondence with Servando Rocha and the publishers La Felquera in Madrid and the Canaries, who had requested information on King Mob and those times long gone. For once we felt the presence of intelligent probing, cutting through the crap. Normally we wouldn't have responded to such requests, as over the past decades most of them have been on the lines of requesting journalistic interviews or concerned with aspects of image/media rebellion we have no interest in whatsoever.

Newcastle

By 1967, as art students in Newcastle-upon-Tyne, we were actively critiquing much of the local cultural scene; slowly and hesitantly proclaiming the supersession and transcendence of art. The hub of the Beat scene in Newcastle was the Morden Tower, a medieval construct abutting Hadrian's Wall, which ran through the heart of Newcastle. After London, it was the essential stop over for American Beat poets visiting the UK, and Allen Ginsberg was a regular visitor. The people who ran this unofficial arts centre were regularly in trouble with the police (usually for smoking dope) and were permanently unemployed, exploiting a loophole in social security laws that allowed them, as unemployed poets, to claim the dole (as there was no work for poets on Tyneside). The cheek, of course, was admirable and attracted dissident working class youth who then cynically used the label 'artist' just to stay on the dole unmolested, and free therefore to laze around all day. Attached to the Morden Tower project was the alternative bookshop in the nearby Handyside Arcade, *Ultima Thule*; the name of which referenced the wretched Tolkien. Ultima Thule was rather more subversive than its London counterparts such as Gandalf`s Garden (another Tolkein reference) because it was not quite a petite-bourgeois business; many of the books on sale having been stolen from Newcastle's big bookstores like the Students Bookshop just around the corner. Many of the people around Modern Tower professed anarchist sympathies and could be found on soap boxes in the local Bigg Market or Town Moor proclaiming the virtues of anarchism and swearing heartily, causing the police on duty to upbraid them for their immoderate language. A semantic, often very funny discussion would then ensue as to what was meant by the term swearing and the air would turn even bluer! However, 'culture' would get the better of this very promising scene and by the late 1970s there was nothing left of it. Its leading representative, the poet Tom Pickard, had become a respectable, suited, journalist writing for local newspapers under the pseudonym Mouth of the Tyne (i.e. a pun on bigmouth as well as Tynemouth). By this time Newcastle was just beginning to redefine itself as the city of installation art, picking up from where we had left off, though absolutely shorn of any revolutionary content and far more socially conservative than the more traditional, counter-cultural, art scene it was rapidly supplanting.

Newcastle was never a backwater and there is every reason to think that the idea of the general strike first originated there, sometime around the 1830s, described as the 'grand national holiday', imbuing the notion with an air of festivity which reappeared in the late 1960s. It was an area also marked by the most bitter industrial disputes particularly in the coalmines. The miners of Chopgate (pronounced Chopyat) just south of Newcastle, went on strike during the 1920s for over three years, at one point threatening to blow up the mine like in a rerun of Zola's Germinal, - though crucially this time without the involvement of an outside agitator. To survive some of the miners lived in the woods foraging for berries and snaring rabbits, or connies as they were referred to. They were following the example of their ancestors in the 19th century, who also dug makeshift homes in the ground when evicted from their cottages by the coal owners during a strike. Curiously, Newcastle was Luis Bunuel's favourite fantasy city, and though he never visited it he liked to dream about it. Perhaps he saw something in it we did not. Though traumatised by the place, unable to return even for a visit and despite our exile, it still exerts a grip on us.

New York

In the summer of 1967, two of us (Anne Ryder and David Wise) specifically chose to go to New York to meet Black Mask. It proved to be an eye-opener and quite an experience, which changed our lives forever. We went from Newcastle to New York via a London airport. Being very young, we had in a sense by-passed London and we were in fact disdainful of the London-centred 'counter culture' promoted by *International Times*.

Newcastle was a city of intense contrasts, not so much between rich and poor as we see today in say, Sao Paulo, but between revolutionary 'theoretical' workers like the brilliant Jack Common and a bourgeoisie who would prefer to reach for the gun rather than negotiate. During the General Strike of 1926, the bourgeoisie in Newcastle armed themselves against the workers more than in any other comparable city in the country. As we have learnt to our cost, reaction always packed a punch in Newcastle and an air of suppressed violence was a constant feature of Newcastle life. So in a sense going to New York in 1967 was like home from home and I can remember sitting on a side walk one unbearably hot summer night and being more or less unfazed by a youth who passed by, casually smashing windows to either side of us as he did so. Just like Newcastle I thought to myself.

Ben Morea was impressed by my relaxed attitude. I then explained to him something of the area's history as outlined briefly above. Yes, we fitted in just fine and dandy with Ron, Janice, Yvonne, Ben and co on the Lower East Side in New York. There was also a profound social connection. We instantly recognised each other as having come from the lower end of the shit heap. We were quite spontaneously maladjusted. with nonetheless sufficient clued-in 'middle class' knowledge to get the authorities sufficiently disturbed when in our presence.

Looking back, Black Mask was, in many respects, more precise and rigorous than the Motherfuckers, as the latter tended to fall into super-militancy with a strong overlay of active mysticism as hippie transformed itself into yippie. Yet many of the Black Mask interventions were indeed excellent and Ben still displays a dislike of superficiality a la Jerry Rubin! We also met Alan Hoffmann; though in 1967 Alan was something of a wet drop out. Ben Morea could barely tolerate him and said so to his face. At the same time, Alan couldn't keep away from Ben and seemed to welcome his brickbats. A short while later he would become the target of Raoul Vaneigem's censure for asking him if his *Totality for Kids* (which is how his *Banalities de Base* had been translated into English) applied to the kids on other planets. Vaneigem objected to Hoffman's mysticism though many, particularly older New Yorkers like Murray Bookchin, were rather more tolerant of it, finding in it a source of amusement. For instance, someone calling up to him from the street outside had awakened Alan one night. Thinking it was God calling him he had gone to the window to ask what God wanted of him! A year and a half later he was to figure large in the Motherfuckers. Remember though, that something of the 'mystical' disposition was also a reflection of indigenous American hunter-gatherer practices which were finally receiving something of the attention they richly deserved, an attention which is today even more necessary than in the late 1960s.

Interestingly, Ben Morea was to say in 2007, almost as if he was confusing himself with Alan's identity: 'I was once accused by Guy Debord of being too mystical….can one be too mystical. Didn't he become his own spectacle?' Well, there is also sufficient truth in the latter comment, even though the mystical content in us, 'the difficult, fucking Wise twins', is virtually zilch.

You may gather from the above how lively the street scene then was in this area of New York. In Ben's company we were constantly bumping into and talking to people. There was a rigour about it and anyone who copped out was denounced. I recall how Ed Sanders of The Fugs pop group covered his face when he saw us and ran away, too ashamed to talk. His face had recently appeared on the cover of *Time* magazine. Instead of jumping for joy he'd got maudlin drunk and in his cups repeated over and over again 'I've sold out, I've sold out'. He knew only too well he had been *recuperated*, though in New York that word had nothing like the resonance it then had in France. And he knew he could expect nothing but the harshest criticism from the people he most wanted respect from.

(How different it all is from today when pandering to the now fully-fledged, dumb and dumber, celebrity culture passes without a word of rebuke. The only other comparable occasion that comes to mind over the past thirty years involves Joe Strummer of The Clash who lived close by us in London. He also used to look away embarrassed whenever we encountered him in the street, casting his eyes to the ground. To tell the truth we were surprised he even knew of us, so great was the gap now developing between the new aristocracy of rock stars - even those that purported to want a revolution like Strummer - and us no-marks below.)

In 1970 in San Francisco I met Alan Hoffman just before he was accidentally killed falling out of the back of a van. By this time he had become heavily critical of the Motherfuckers, accusing the group of aggressive militant image-making that was impossible to live up to for any length of time. He could see it was leading to a catastrophic nervous breakdown amongst Ben's followers, who were rapidly making him into an object of hero worship. With two women in tow he would, according to Alan, tout his rifle like he was living out a Hollywood biopic on Zapata or Pancho Villa, striking poses that the police might take only too real pot shots at. I readily recognised what Alan was saying as I'd recently met a Motherfucker in London who had modelled himself on Ben Morea: even deploying the same gestures and accent! I think it was Alan who mentioned how one

Motherfucker had gone completely crazy threatening to throw himself off Brooklyn Bridge, screaming he was 'being consumed by the Motherfuckers'. It certainly gave a new twist to the critique of spectacular consumption.

This pressurised consumption of revolutionary images would shortly find an even more suffocating expression in the counter revolutionary, Maoist orientated, Weathermen (and women), no matter what you can say about them on other levels. Feeling like awkward, clumsy, weak rejects, we felt totally alienated from these tendencies, sensing with dread a marked decline in the spontaneous, very creative flow/explosion of the late 1960s; though as yet we hardly dared to say so, as the revolutionary critique of much (though not all) terrorism was only then in the process of taking shape. At the same time it seemed Ben was also unable to carry on with the rebel pose and, almost in a flash, was to dissolve his image and disappear for decades.

Alan, though, was still the zany mystic it seemed he'd always been. This had not prevented him in the meantime from becoming a martial arts expert, saying he'd 'got his guns stashed for the days of insurrection' that were to come. He then handed me a long and convoluted poster decorated in the margins with coloured ying and yang type drawings. It also contained a dense eco sub-text I just couldn't get my head around. Couched in a vague, woolly, even ethereal language about the complexities of present day rural communes in America, it was like a Walt Whitman poem gone dreadfully wrong, minus too, William Blake's crude down-to-earth penetrating insights. It wasn't that I was then opposed to eco-critique; I just thought this type of approach unhelpful, as I couldn't really make out what was being said.

Alan was also a friend of Murray Bookchin, who was, of course, always making his presence felt. Much the older man, he would readily go out of his way to encourage these young revolutionaries. He certainly brought with him a profound and original ecological critique that was way ahead of anything in

Europe at that time. The problem was that he tended to confuse ecological initiatives with small businesses like whole food cafes, etc, which were then just beginning to appear, particularly in an agriculturally devastated parts of America. Commendably, though he was later to attack this capitalisation, he was then at a loss to understand how people did not feel liberated in these highly self conscious, holier than thou, eateries. In fact most of us felt rather more aggressive inside them than we would in a hamburger joint as if there was something not quite wholesome about them; their sole purpose being to sweep the real problems under the carpet.

Murray in fact rebuked ex-King Mobbist, Phil Mailer (who was seven years later to write in 1976 *The Impossible Revolution* on the social uprising in Portugal 1974-76) for not being awestruck when taken to see the Grand Canyon. Phil could only feel dead inside like he was viewing a Hollywood stage set. When he apologetically told the nonplussed Murray about his feelings it was like he was confessing, wretch that he was, to an (Irish) sin, though at the same time enjoying the discomfort he was causing.

We liked Murray enormously as a person. He was always warm and friendly and would readily shake your hand as though he meant it. In retrospect we do wish he'd talked and written more about his past involvement in car factory and railway workers' strikes because before he entered the academic arena he'd been 'a working stiff' (i.e. corpse), as they say in America. It would have been fascinating stuff, though we do know he regretted not running away to Spain at the age of 16 in 1936-37 to join *Los Incontrolados*. It seemed he couldn't forgive himself for this. As he had been barely in his mid- teens back then no one criticised him for allowing himself to be talked out of going to fight for the Spanish Revolution. However, we would all grow a trifle weary of his never ending, erudite, conversation; one of the Californians from the pro-situ group *Contradiction* wittily referred to him - with his academic role in mind - as 'Murray Bookshelf'.

Included here is a leaflet from my time in New York in 1967 called Freedom is not a gift from Captain Fink which was one of the best Black Mask flyers ever put out on the streets. It's never been reproduced anywhere simply because it was lost and I only found it recently in a pile of mucky papers in my bedroom. (Actually most of the BM/Motherfucker material published in English came from similar mucky piles in my London flat and not from New York - much to the amusement of some Americans). Fresh out of Newcastle, I actually had a small hand in composing the Captain Fink flyer while sitting around a big, old wooden table in Ben's very sparsely furnished, not to say austere, apartment on the Lower East Side. Captain Fink was the new top cop of the local precinct and in a way represented the changing face of policing in strife-torn America. Fink opted for a more manipulative approach rather than deploy the usual heavy-handed tactics of shoot first and ask questions afterwards. It was this more sophisticated, controlling approach that the flyer condemned.

All well and good but actually it was a different story when four or five of us handed the leaflet out in the streets. I remember attending a large Black Power meeting on the Lower East Side to listen to H. Rap Brown who was speaking inside a large building, which was already full to overflowing. So many people had turned up that the streets around the building were jam packed mainly with Afro-Caribbeans, though there were a few palefaces amongst the throng. On the flat roofs of the surrounding high 19th century brownstone buildings there were occasional machine gun posts (courtesy of Captain Fink?) manned by police units, with the barrels of the machine guns pointing directly down into the crowds (remember this was just after the huge urban riots in Newark and Detroit). With my heart in my mouth I started handing out the Captain Fink leaflet together with other Black Mask stuff. Suddenly two cops jumped me, one thrusting a gun in my ribs whilst the other shoved the barrel of his gun against my forehead. They seized what I was carrying and slyly pilfered personal belongings though they stopped short of doing anything else. At the same moment another cop sidled up to Anne, who was wearing a mini-skirt, (English mini-skirts were still much shorter than their American counterparts) kissing her full on the lips. Obviously I was shaken as previous run-ins with police in the north of England had been nothing like this. I was certain at the very least I'd be immediately deported back to England but the cops didn't seem interested and perhaps assumed I was American. The personal humiliation was enough and once over with they laid off. The Black guys around me looked on quizzically and, if anything, were a wee bit flummoxed as if not knowing what to make of it all. Ben Morea though, had witnessed the whole incident and came running up just as the cops were moving on. He shook his head and said; 'Dave, you shouldn't have let them take the leaflets'! It was then the difference between Newcastle and New York really struck home. But let's take a look at what the leaflet said:

Freedom is not a gift from Captain Fink

The hippies have become victims of their own ideology. In their rejection of the grand spectacle 'Hollywood/Madison Ave./America' they have accepted a spectacle no less destructive, one which substitutes synthetic play for real life, while at the same time they have become tools of those against whom they have supposedly rebelled. They have added to the rostrum of 'stars' who entertain the corpse of the bourgeoisie, a corpse which seeks to remake the world in its own image.

Baby, you haven't dropped out, you've been forced out because this goddamn system is rotten. But what they will never allow is for us to remake our lives, because that will signal their end: they must instead either attempt to either recoup our revolt by making it into a spectacle which reaffirms their vitality while it drains ours or they will seek to crush us. And we must fight either. This one by refusing to "play their games" while real life is denied, the other by open struggle. "If they want to play Nazis, we ain't going to play Jews". And so our struggle crosses that of the blacks and together we can tear this shit down.

The American Indian was forced onto reservations (concentration camps) he did not retire there to smoke and groove. Life cannot be limited to a 'reserve' specified by those who seek to control us. We must decide where and when we will live, play or die, otherwise our freedom is a lie.

This swirling vortex suggestive of a hurricane, with the word NOW stamped across it, was imprinted on the back of the leaflet. For anyone with half an eye the avant-garde associations were immediately obvious and could have come straight out of the annals of Dadaism or Futurism, though all the more powerful through being put to use in a very real context and as far from the polite world of museums as it was possible to be. Remember too that museums had been the target of the first issue of Black Mask, to the consternation of a number of Murray Bookchin's followers. More specifically, it betrayed Ben's original love for Abstract Expressionism especially the work of Jackson Pollock. I had in fact been keen on Jackson Pollock myself in my late teens but during the recent *Icteric* years in Newcastle had distanced myself more and more from AE (as we called it), regarding the movement as a retarded artistic recuperation of more promising anti-art tendencies in the Surrealist movement. Pollock was a sort of psychic automatism in paint, which stopped far short of taking the next step into the arena of everyday life as the surrealists had done in their random walks. Though on a very different plain to the more socially attuned derives many years later, they were an anticipation of them in so far as they left the studio and the writing desk behind. For me AE art was nothing other than better-quality wallpaper. Ben and I talked about all of this as we drifted about here, there and everywhere in New York and he'd agreed with me only to end up with: 'But, goddamn it Dave, I still love Jackson Pollock.'

A few years later I was to learn of a comical follow-up to this. Bruce Elwell, an American member of the original Situationist International, recalled to mind heated conversations he had with Ben around the same time, which focussed on that huge swathe of industry on the outskirts of New York, called the New Jersey Turnpike. Bruce wanted to see a Salvador Dali type melting process taking over these oil refineries and storage depots whilst Ben wanted them to remain much as they were, with maybe a little more angularity and straight lines - an Americanised revolutionary equivalent of Russian constructivism if you like. Duchamp during his long sojourn in America had said something like 'as for art, America has its plumbing and bridges'. Perhaps Ben had really taken this observation to heart. We can today laugh at the earnestness of this exchange but the laugh will be on us if we fail to recognize what has been lost. Stemming from the fundamental recognition of the need for a revolution, what was commendable about these two different approaches was their visionary impulse, which was profoundly orientated to taking possession of all objects around us.

In retrospect, all this raises a number of points that for too long have been glossed over. Ben and I had a number of things in common like our fairly recent background in art, racing from that into an anti-art perspective and then, in short order, into a revolutionary one (coincidentally, in order to survive, Ben and Ron Hahn also did painting and decorating as well as window cleaning). All this had occurred within the space of two years, three years at the maximum. We never really mentioned this to each other; it was almost as if as if we were ashamed to do so, as we were profoundly embarrassed - and I do mean profoundly embarrassed - by our juvenilia and former naivety. We put on the airs of a modern revolutionary sophistication far in advance of our understanding and experience, one that fell far short of a genuine subversive awareness able to withstand the shocks (and how!) that were shortly to come. On the other hand our overwhelming eagerness to get out there and do things compensated for this lack, and the urgency of the times led us to think the future was within our grasp, a future we were going to fundamentally shape.

A similar suppression of the immediate past was also evident a little later in the early days of King Mob (e.g. Chris Gray had been involved in Indica gallery Happenings only a year and a half previously). As for me (or rather ourselves) we'd been involved in the then 'unmentionable' *Icteric* experiment in Newcastle, blushing at the mention of the name.

One of the last projects before *Icteric* fell apart - as it had to under the pressure of these revolutionary times - had been a utopian architectural scheme we'd put together in miniature marquette form which we then photographed in a bog in the Northumbrian countryside just north of Newcastle. We are still embarrassed at the mere thought of it but this whimsical utopian construct of straw roofed cardboard huts with mad stairs reaching up into star-lit heavens had been loosely based on the *Voyage to Laputa* in Jonathan Swift's *Gulliver's Travels*, as well as reference to the postman Cheval's fairy palace at Hauterive in France and ad hoc 'primitive' constructions in general. The *Voyage to Laputa* was easily the most fire-cracker section of *Gulliver's Travels*, Swift's invective knowing no bounds, even satirising without mercy the august Royal Society of his day so recently ruled over by Isacc Newton. In fact we had reproduced a paragraph from Swift in *Icteric* wherein he just about slates every imaginable profession, letting rip with a torrent of breath-taking vituperation. Aware that the surrealists had fulsomely praised Swift for being 'surrealist in irony' we were reading into it a seminal critique of a very modern division of labour which had evolved to the point of complete madness. We also liked the fact that Laputa was a floating island and seemed to be a kind of 'land art' equivalent of Malevich's suprematist space cube.

This utopian scheme had been put together in response to a suggestion by the New York Happener, Dick Higgins, who had circulated a request for just such schemes. Together with Wolf Vostell from the European Fluxus group (co-founded by Higgins in America) he intended to combine them in a book on utopian 'architectural' schemes. In fact, although the book project was flirting with the notion of anti-architecture, typically Higgins preferred to hang on to the term 'architecture'. The book, published by the Something Else Press, finally appeared in

1969 under the title of *Fantastic Architecture*. Possibly he was afraid that if he dropped the term he would be assisting a revolutionary mob that was then pressing at the gates of the city determined to burn it to the ground in order to reconstruct everything anew.

Sometime in the late spring of 1967 Ron Hunt of *Icteric* sent off the photographs and accompanying texts to Higgins. Come summer, however, the bomb of revolution was exploding big time in us and we knew we had little choice but go completely beyond art and the artefact in order to find their realization in the act of total revolution. So we hastily consigned everything we'd done that was leading up to it to the dustbin of history.

A few days after meeting Ben, rather shamefacedly I casually mentioned this scheme in passing. He responded by saying we go and see Higgins who just happened to live around the corner. In any case, he too wanted to see him. We arranged a meeting and visited him, though after a few minutes both of us quickly realised we couldn't get on with the guy. Higgins thought our anti-architectural scheme was 'dreadful' and though he was right about that, it was certainly no worse than any of the others he was to praise in his forthcoming book. Looking back, I think he took exception to the violence of the texts that accompanied the scheme. These were directly aimed at the knuckle-headed, unbelievably philistine stupidity we had run up against in Newcastle.

Higgins appeared to be more interested in Black Mask. A discussion on Cuba ensued with Higgins asking Ben what would he do if he lived there? Ben unhesitatingly replied he would organise a band of people and go back into the Sierra Maestra and from there, armed with a genuinely socially libertarian critique, fight Castro's Bolshevism. (Little did we know but at the time according to anarcho-syndicalist Sam Dolgoff, in his book on Cuba nine years later. some guerrillas had begun to do just that. In response to the industrialisation of agriculture agenda being implemented by the Che Guevara Brigades.)

At one point Alan Kaprow, the well-known New York

Happener, came in and picked up a copy of Black Mask, remarking how beautiful the typography looked. Raising his eyes, Ben shot me a despairing glance. Once outside Higgins's door and back on the street both Ben and I, exasperated beyond measure, started bad-mouthing both of them. We agreed they'd never step outside the framework of installation art and happenings and in this we were proved completely right. Once back in his Lower East Side second floor apartment Ben opened a recent book by Higgins titled *Jefferson's Birthday,* also published by Something Else Press. Going to the page where he said he was about to take to the barricades, he tore it out in fury.

Higgins died in 1997 shortly after his sixtieth birthday. He had been due to attend another pointless Fluxus event he'd been scheduled to speak at. We nearly said inconsequential rather than pointless but that just would not be true because the latter-day influence of Fluxus is bigger than ever. Though immense and growing it is a hidden presence, particularly in the pop music industry. The lead sound engineer D Toop of Bono's band U2, is a Fluxus fan, as is Brian Eno and latterly Johnny Rotten of Sex Pistols fame. Rotten/Lydon has now swapped the art/anti-art posture of a much watered-down situationism he was manipulated into adopting for a far more orthodox Fluxus-inspired one which he fancies he has freely chosen, though in reality he is almost completely ignorant of the origins and history of these drastically opposed movements. The worst aspect of this whole affair is that there is virtually no one around today capable of critiquing this development. To put it baldly, we were - and still are - for intervention and disruption; Fluxus and co for performance and display. And those who should know better now grow angry at the merest mention of this distinction; such is the sacrosanct grip of art over even the best people just at the moment when intelligent subversion is more needed than ever.

At the time I did wonder why Ben wanted to meet Higgins. I got the impression Ben had been an Action Painter a number of years earlier, jacking it the moment his body and soul was gripped by the prospect of a total revolution. But truth to tell, what we were doing in Newcastle was far more negative as regards art than Black Mask's critique; and when we first saw a reproduction of a Henry Moore sculpture on the front page of an edition of Black Mask we automatically assumed it was a piss-take. Soon however it was followed by a Juan Miro illustration and we all began to wonder what the hell was going on.

Years later we realised Ben had followed a similar trajectory to ourselves in Newcastle, only he had reached the finishing post a few months before we had. Ben's winding path to that end had passed through the doors of Julian Beck's and Judith Malina's *Living Theatre* project, which was based on Artaud's *The Theatre of Cruelty*. A little later on and now calling themselves the Motherfuckers, Ben and newfound friends were to occupy the Fillmore East Auditorium, with the intention of turning it into a revolutionary base. In order to stop the cops from invading the building, Ben turned to Julian Beck for assistance, hoping, no doubt, that Beck's reputation on the New York cultural scene would allay the cops. It was almost as if he now had need of Captain Fink's broader cultural grasp.

How much Ben's participation in the Living Theatre project had helped him along the way is a moot point. Certainly, in the not too distant past, he had burst through the sham and ritualised pretence of Performance Art to engage with 'real life'. When I first met him he suggested that being waylaid by the Living Theatre had been nothing but an embarrassing waste of time he would as soon forget about. However the Motherfuckers' kamikaze, ultra-voluntarism could also send him, at short notice, straight into the arms of a recuperation he had turned his back on. No doubt Ben would dispute this, as his street-cred spontaneity and talent for instantaneous direct action could never be doubted. Only afterwards did he wonder how he'd get out of the deepest shite he'd landed himself in.

Interestingly a few months before meeting Ben, a few of us in *Icteric* had, on the spur of the moment, disrupted a Merce Cunningham dance performance in London. I don't know if Ben, unable to tolerate the pretence any longer, had done something similar around the same time. But here at least was an overlap - though one I never thought worth mentioning to Ben, even in passing.

Ben Morea has recently 'returned' to visiting New York on a regular basis from the wilds of New Mexico and now, after all these years of absence, writes a blog called *E-Blast*. Typically Ben, the style tends to the pert and epigrammatic, though perhaps too restricted to politics and not enough about society at large. On the other hand, in a recent interview he explains just how acute his analysis of the late 1960s is. He calls one of us 'a great guy' (thanks but we don't need it) having forgotten the name (DW) and in response we reckon he is still a 'stand-up guy' as the Americans say.

So what happened to Ben? (We were even asked the same question by sympathetic Yanks in the 1970s but we hadn't a clue). It seems that after the Motherfuckers, Ben and Janice spent a long-time in the wilderness of the American south-west living the life style of latter-day indigenous Americans (ye old , avoiding police detection before Ben became a lumberjack and was somewhat invalided by a chainsaw accident. But the myths which arose once he'd disappeared from the rebel 'spotlights' were similarly wild ranging from horse breeder/trader to rich businessman.

Our meeting with Black Mask in New York in 1967 was to have big repercussions vis-à-vis the last days of Icteric in Newcastle. Our encounter was to prove crucial in the break-up of the English section of the International Situationists. Once collaboration all-round really got underway, the English section were left with the unenviable job of trying to explain to Guy Debord, etc, that they had met some people from the far north of England they could get along with and wished to somewhat hold fire regarding critique of emerging ex-Black Mask/Motherfucker activities. The French were entirely justified in pointing to the latter's hotchpotch character, such as uncritical support for the philosopher Bertrand Russell's US war crimes appeals, and publishing an interview with Albert Camus. Though we could not doubt the general superiority of the Situationist International critique emanating from France we also knew that in America and the UK, especially the latter, we were virtually starting out from scratch with very, very little in our immediate past we could fall back on as inspiration and guidance. We were floundering as well as making real advances.

Theoretical Reflections

It is only now that the connections, which were then very opaque because of a shared abhorrence regarding our immediate past, are becoming apparent. Many of us around that time had very quickly passed through this latter day, decadent, cultural avant-gardism to the easy embrace of the need for a total revolution that would *realize* art, a project first astonishingly flagged by Hegel over 140 years previously. I say 'easy' because that step then seemed so very logical and we were at a loss to understand why others, like the Fluxus troupe, could not see it as blindingly obvious. However the latter were to prove the easy victors in this contest, and the status of the avant-garde in the last forty years moved from the margins to occupy centre stage. This process rapidly accelerated after the turn of the millennium, with the path to revolutionary transcendence becoming totally cut off.

It now behoves all of us to try and explain why this radical, very necessary development has come to a full stop, and why especially now we can begin to speak of an aesthetic political economy in which the wall of money was to prove ultimately decisive. We need to link it to the hegemony of finance capital in the west and the rise of industrially subcontracted nations like China in particular, and, to a lesser extent, India. This new fangled aesthetic economy, still very much in the making, has everything to do with asset inflation, itself dependent on the credit mechanism and the easy availability of money for those who can use their appreciating assets, like avant-garde art, as collateral. Inevitably an economy like this devalues labour, with the working class, regarded, in some quarters at least, as the *salt* of the earth, becoming the *scum* of the earth.

More crucially, this development undermines, though by no means fatally, Marx's labour theory of value to such an extent that those who rigidly adhere to it become insensible to what is different in this most dire of situations. A Political Economy of Art was first advanced by John Ruskin in the 19th century; and in retrospect it does seem more than strange that neither Marx nor Engels paid the slightest attention to it. In fact Ruskin's *Political Economy of Art* was firmly grounded in Ricardo's theory of labour value and was based on the honest, enduring, value of craft-based production, like stone carving, that had remained unchanged for centuries and therefore clashed fundamentally with the surfeit of constantly de-valorising products issuing from the mechanised factories. It is a concept of little relevance in today's aesthetic economy, though one has to acknowledge Ruskin's perspicacity in raising the possibility of a political economy of art. Though affirming the spirit of labour and the correct frame of mind prior to the execution of a practical task, Ruskin's economy is in fact a very material one, carrying far more weight than today's corporeal 'weightless economy'. However these phantoms, though very real values, float on as the very opposite to today's ruling conceptual art and the process of valorisation it is utterly dependent on - like the machinery of publicity rather than factory production, personal reputation rather than actual product.

Perhaps if Marx and Engels had deigned to consider Ruskin's views they may well have remembered the German idealist philosophy of their youth and in particular the major importance given to aesthetics in the systems of Kant, Fichte, Schelling and Hegel. By relating that concern to the political economy of their day, Marx and Engels could have made the subject vastly more relevant to the present. Instead they relegated the consideration of aesthetics to the fine arts, a very traditional thing to do and one which, compared to their philosophical predecessors, marked a major step backwards.

Aesthetics today is, of course, a dirty word and we can barely comprehend how 200 years ago it had become linked, through the auspices of German philosophical idealism, to the practical historical action Marx was at pains to emphasize, and which had been so sorely neglected by French and English materialism.

Having more than glanced through Marx's *Capital,* particularly *Volume One* and the chapters devoted to an analysis of the labour process as transformed by modern inventions like steam powered machinery, we have for a number of years now been struck by the absence of any mention of photography in the combined oeuvre of Marx and Engels. More than ever, it seems a great oversight. Surely Engels, who survived Marx by a good few years, must have been aware of its growing importance to capitalism, particularly the photo-litho process essential to the production of newspapers and posters, from which eventually would spring today's miles of advertising hoardings. It is rather revealing to think that task was left to Mallarme, one of the first tentative anti-poets, to begin to unravel.

The ramifications of finance capital today - hedge funds, private equity funds, house price inflation, advertising, auctions, etc, - always raise, either directly or indirectly, the issue of art somewhere along the line. Here in the UK, even more than New York or America in general, it is hardly possible to switch on the TV or open a newspaper without being confronted with yet another yawningly empty manifestation of avant-garde art, masking the fact that even the bourgeois democracy we have become accustomed to over the past century is everywhere on the retreat. It is a situation that is rotten ripe for revolt but so far, incredibly, there is not the slightest sign of this happening. On a positive note, all we can say is that when it does - and we fervently hope it will be soon - the bourgeoisie will not be ready for it, lulled as they are, increasingly thanks to avant-garde art, into complacency without precedent.

In the meantime we must remorselessly critique our pasts and those who wish to keep us stuck fast within them. Any kind of fame is useless to all of us. All our pasts must be subjected to perceptive critique preparing the way, yet again, to hopefully getting the world out of a rapidly descending inferno far worse than anything we combated in the late 1960s and, which we were severely punished for. There is no point in emptily affirming reified images.

Getting By

The experience and memory of King Mob and its immediate off-shoots has never gone away in Britain and Ireland, despite much mythologizing, dreadful interpretations, resentful denigrations and laudings. Nobody belonging to the original movements has, in anything like depth - apart from ourselves (Dave & Stu' Wise) - commented much on what took place and, in some ways more importantly, what happened afterwards. Thus, it appears that everything has vanished from historical interpretation apart from ever-reoccurring logos on T-shirts and empty images. We feel that this is related to appalling compromises many of the individuals involved made as means and mode of survival in their daily lives.

As for ourselves, our late website *Revolt Against Plenty* explored the King Mob movement and its precursor, the *Icteric* experiment, in Newcastle-upon-Tyne. Our unfinished and incomplete, notes were put together in haste at a time of near absolute hell when death was beckoning on two fronts: one concerned grave physical illness; the other, which included a few others - brave guys and gals - who lived at the sharp end without role or status, involved having to take on heavily-capitalised and armed drug gangs who'd made life impossible in the social housing complexes we occupied. Our effective action against these brutalised crack dealers meant, on the word of the grapevine, that there were contracts out on us. The police, housing authorities and local Labour Party MPs were more than happy about this as we'd been forced to take on these intermediaries as well, with a full frontal of stinging analysis in letters and leaflets. (We won't list here some of the direct action tactics - for obvious reasons - we deployed against the dealers though they were very effective).

As a way of making certain that many decades of thoughts, documents and diaries meant something a flood of memories erupted in the shape of *The Hidden History of King Mob* (written by David Wise, though twin brother has still fought shy of making a contribution and no doubt, a stern auto-critique).

King Mob in Britain partook of a moment and movement - that of the original Situationist critique - which should have been far greater than the rebellion of modern art and, much further back, of the revolutionary romanticism that existed before and after the fulcrum of the French revolution of 1789. Romantic revolt in Britain was, if anything, the wildest and most splendid of international responses. We have written about it in a somewhat tongue-in-cheek, academic kind of way to provoke those dead relics of nothingness, the university lecturers.

The shock waves from the revolt of the late 1960s took a long time to ebb, especially in the UK, which idiosyncratically just seemed to keep on going and going up to the Poll Tax riots of 1990 and even, a little later with the anti-road protestors; but the razor sharp edge of profound critical incision was blunted very quickly. As Ron Hunt of *Icteric* in Newcastle put it at the time, 'The avant-garde of hope has given way to the avant-garde of despair'. Breakdown and depression quickly followed suit engulfing a fair number in suicide.

Needless to say, police pressure and fingering by state security personnel didn't help in this mix. Personal, sexual relationships foundered, often giving vent to terrible recriminations and inter-personal nastiness. We all went mad with sheer agony. In retrospect, these horrific experiences were also something you had to go through simply to understand something of the agonising depths of experience, of real life, 'of the minds other kingdom', as Shakespeare put it. Though naively, even superficially, we'd learnedly quoted the horror and illusive transcendence inherent in the writings of Lautreamont, there was something far too stylish about it when most of us had yet to personally encounter the depths of Maldoror's inferno. Rightly, at this moment of this self-realisation, TJ Clark of King Mob produced a small, vituperative pamphlet, which got the Sunday tabloid *News of the World* baying for his blood. The pamphlet reversed De Sade's loudly proclaimed slogan of the time: 'Nihilists one more effort to be revolutionaries' into: 'Revolutionaries one more effort to be nihilists'. This acute reversal was in response to the fact that everywhere you turned there seemed to be individuals spouting revolutionary phrase-mongering that simply sounded hollow. The trouble was that although our TJ had made a correct diagnostic it was also a self-analysis.

Despair bred obedience but, paradoxically, at the heart of the rejection of money a love of money was rekindled from dying embers. It was to turn into an imperious lust the likes of which, as time went by, we've never ever historically previously experienced. To continue in our subversive quest, a course, a *passage,* inherited perhaps from previous *derives*, had been roughly envisaged if not accurately mapped-out. Fundamentally, it meant the abandonment of all professional roles such as artist, writer, poet, architect or academic, along with all the rest of what could be taken as cadre roles buttressing the dominant ideology. We - echoing Rimbaud's exhortations in *A Season in Hell* - had necessarily to be very severe with ourselves. With no immediate sign of a revolutionary breakthrough on the horizon it was a tall order and hardly surprisingly that all of us - ourselves included - twisted and turned at the implications. Surely one could work a couple of days per week lecturing on some crap or hang out as a nondescript, part time town planner? Simply be a bit knowingly cynical about survival? Alas, alas it doesn't work out like that. There was no escape; you had to journey on downwards and the path to eternity as Nietzsche had said, 'is bent', though we weren't sure what 'bent' meant and probably Nietzsche wasn't too sure of that either, though he was clearly pointing in the right direction.

The rebellion against art and all other manifest alienations such as the family, monogamy, religion and work, gave way to a much more fundamental, day to day, agonised survival; a thoroughly proletarianised reality of knowing you had no dosh to fall back upon. You began to hate the fact the majority of your former privileged King Mob 'comrades' from the middle or, upper middle classes, gradually made some agonised peace with their backgrounds, slowly distancing themselves from your vulgar reality, finally disappearing altogether into safer niches and the latest tranche of inherited wealth, which this time they firmly kept glued in their pockets. Finally though, you hated even more those from your own poor backgrounds who, seeing clearly the hypocrisy of their former friends, simply made a play for the crudest means of making vast amounts of money.

Some individuals didn't compromise, but with the increasing fragmentation caused by the community breakdown and urban dispersal, they found themselves bit by bit in a state of limbo. Without profile, though remaining fine people, they were increasingly finding their rebel spirit smashed to smithereens. None of this need have happened. Even though, by ourselves, we couldn't have stopped the advance and domination of finance capitalism, we could have at least continued to make a mark, giving the system lucid scares. 'Every Little Helps' as the Tesco supermarket ad goes. We also could, on a more collective level, have kept the perspective of total social revolution and the transformation of everyday life alive and kicking so that others, much younger, could have taken up cudgels en-route to more definitive and happier conclusions.

It wasn't so much that the revolutionary critique of art was left behind; rather it was waylaid at the time by more basic considerations, as you were forced to be part of the movement from below, pushing towards conflict with the trade union apparatus and a growing statist-oriented community politics increasingly ensconced in the broader arena of issue politics.

KING MOB: THE NEGATION AND TRANSCENDENCE OF ART

Inevitably though there was no arena to turn to which you could feel at home in, either that of Trotskyism or traditional anarchism or the growing ultra left like World Revolution and the neo-Bordigists who were so reductive, throwing their constant absolutes at you like a chant.

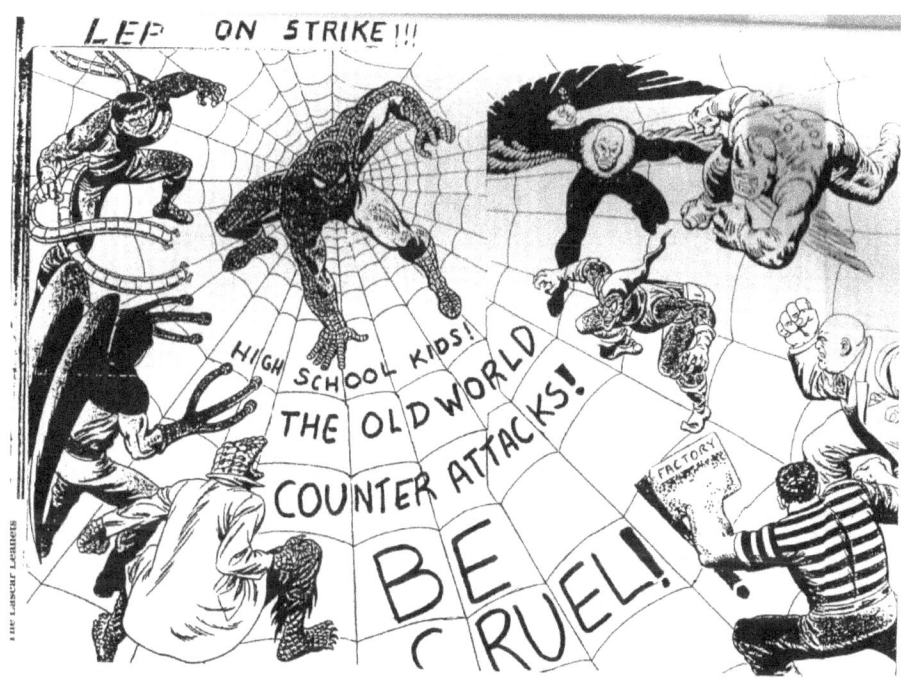

(Lacar Apprentices strike leaflet)

For us working in construction, hatred of sub-contractors in the building industry reigned supreme together with an eye for all the un-named acts of revolt which happen on a day-to-day basis, never receiving official recognition. These acts are the warp and woof; endlessly reinvigorating the failing sense of life imposed by re-invigorated, now missionary-like, powers that be. The yearning for revolution never diminished; rather it re-established something of its essence in the communal relations and often exhilarating antics which began to affect the things you wrote when the urge came upon - as much as you held in disdain - and rightly so - the role of writer.

Around the time of great strike wave of the Winter of

Discontent in 1979, Michel Prigent, who was intimately then connected to Guy Debord, suggested that, seeing we had no money and wanted to publish a number of things, we should become sub-contractors and mini-capitalists in the building trade to fund these efforts. It was meant well but it was the one thing we couldn't do, as at that point, unadorned, utterly loyal comradeship on the building site was all we had left of a wrecked personal life. If we'd betrayed that, if we'd betrayed friends seeing we always worked together on the principal of equal wages, we may well have topped ourselves. Fuck the revolutionary theory let someone with real dosh pay for that!

The great urban riots of 1981 hit us like a welcome blow to the head, clearing away so much of the tedious procedurialism that dogs day to day conflict in the workaday world. It was also thirteen years after King Mob had taken its name from the Gordon Riots of 1780 when London had previously been put to the rioters' sword and the slogan King Mob appeared on the walls of the smouldering wreck of Newgate prison. Inevitably with passion and with this in mind, in *Like A Summers With A Thousand Julys* we wrote about this great subversive event. We hoped the riots would spill over into the work scene which in some ways they did especially during the big printers and miners' strike of the following years. All this you could say was very basic stuff though we never once forgot, no matter how pushed into the background, the recuperative role culture played via a growing media circus playing in the background. Beyond that you patiently watched, waiting for renewed youthful bursts in the manner and lucidity of the best of late 1960s King Mob - though we hoped they would be rather better than our own paltry efforts - and a force disrupting on a grander scale than ever, beginning with the cultural perspective. Alas, so far it has never happened.

And then everything was vanquished as the neoliberal counter-revolution really set in. All revolt was wiped out and the best of the most combative element of 'the working class' destroyed through drink, drugs, madness, raving isolation, despair and slow motion suicide (when it wasn't simply the deft slitting of beckoning wrists). Some of our dearest friends departed down these pathways to Hades leaving us only with ghostly memories haunting the rest of our days as a face in the crowd becomes yet again a John Dennis or Pam Smith followed by a desperate cry from within your own heart.

The final twist was to be strange, very strange indeed, as almost everything you'd done, every route you'd opened up especially in your youth around Icteric and King Mob was thrown back in your face as intensifying commodification. But this aesthetic economy is one of constantly moving images, of advertising as endless intervention and seeming disruption, of neoliberal economics disguised as green art installation, of invention become not exhilarating phantasy buta permanent sinister lie. All so reminiscent on the surface of King Mob yet minus the essential.

2 - KING MOB AT SELFRIDGES, DECEMBER 1968

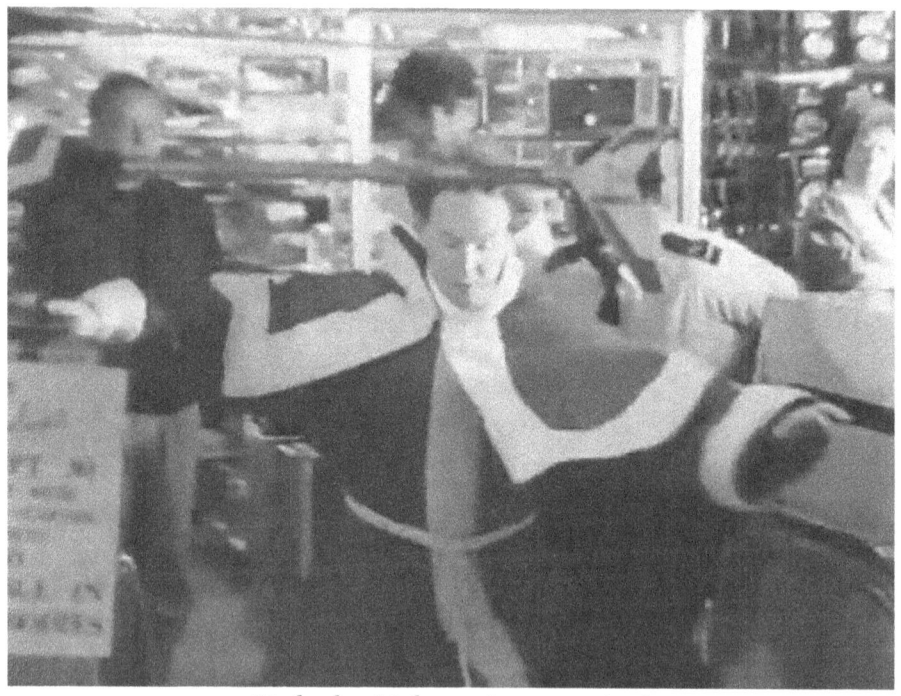

Malcolm Mclaren 're-enacting'

Letter On What Happened at Selfridges Store
Dave Wise
2007

Dear Vicki,

I just wanted to explain a little more about the anti-Xmas, anti-consumer intervention so that you may be able to correct the false assumptions of Jamie Reid [Malcom Mclaren's 'art consultant' for the Sex Pistols 'Swindle' and co-author with Chris Gray of *Leaving the Twentieth Century*]. And I hope he doesn't get annoyed with you about it! He in fact quite recently put on a display in a shop window in Westbourne Grove, Notting Hill for Pepe jeans. It was simple consumer advertising but deployed a lot of his old props like the Boredom and Nowhere destination buses he gleaned from *Point Blank* (a very early 1970s pro-situ group based in San Francisco along with Ken Knabb's *Contradiction*).

After some rudimentary planning in early December 1968 I informed Malcolm Maclaren and Fred Vermorel about what we - King Mob - intended doing and asked if they could they get plenty of people along to Oxford St. By that time I was very friendly with both of them and they listened a lot to what I had to say, which meant I could go on and on and on. I ranged all over, putting forward my theories on English romanticism, English philistinism conjoined to British imperialism, Yorkshire and the north east, plus my knowledge of Russian Constructivism, Surrealism, International Lettrism and the like. Much of the latter – apart from Lettrism – had though come from Ron Hunt in Newcastle.

Fred Vermorel was more clued in about tendencies within the workers' movement. He knew about and could discuss the Friends of Durrutti and the antics of the different Trotskyist sects, etc. In that sense he was very 'French'; his mother hailed from France and of course Fred had fought splendidly on the barricades in Paris in May 1968. None the less, Malcolm Maclaren with his dash and audacity proved to be very plucky and imaginative, darting here, there and everywhere during the battle for Selfridges. (Ashamed to say, I utterly wallowed in the way these two guys listened so attentively. It was very flattering). From an exciting and fulfilled childhood amongst the northern coalfields I too in Newcastle had become very French!

I know Maclaren was particularly fascinated with the concept of the drift, t*he derive.* That allowed me to take-off, not only about Baudelaire but also De Quincey and his influence on Charles Dickens's endless walks through London. The old urban rookeries fascinated MacLaren (Incidentally one of the most haunting descriptions of Liverpool is conjured up by De Quincey as he sits in a room for days on end top of Everton hill looking down on the harbour and listening to all the foreign voices stoned out of his head, motionless on laudanum, or as De Quincey's children delightfully called it "doddenum"!) Later, much later, MM made an arse of all this in his ill-digested attempt to play for Lord Mayor of London with his programmed version of a drift through cultural events, museums and the like.

The Selfridges intervention was really a disparate, collective effort. No one at the time really thought it was something to be claimed, something to be copyrighted for. In any case, that was the enlightened *no property* spirit of the times. Later Maclaren was to say he was dressed as Santa Claus, which wasn't true. A good friend, Peter 'Ben' Trueman, out of his head on speed, did that! In the Oxford St film (*The Ghosts of Christmas Past*) Maclaren voiceovers the leaflet we gave out, but it was the Cleggs and myself who wrote that and then I 'designed' it, making it into a spoof Christmas card kind of thing. Maclaren was certainly in awe of the guy.

Ben was spectacularised by all the recuperated radicals who were essentially using him as thesis material for advancing their future careers. It was as if the guy was the pure essence of uneducated, wild, pristine hooligan revolt, hailing from a working class background in Winchester. *Never a student.* Ah wonderful! Ben was no fool though, and rapidly realised he was being used and even set up. We became excellent friends and had some great times in the pub where he liked to drop a vibrator in pints of beer and watch it froth all over the table - to much hilarity. He was a builder too, though half the time you wondered if he was casing the joint or the church next door where he'd nick the lead off the roof. (This happened!) Around about 1974 I was working with him on a site. It was Xmas Eve (again!) and the boss, after faithfully promising all of us we'd get paid on the dot at 5 in the evening, came up and told us he had no money. Ben knocked him out with a heavy left to the jaw and then proceeded to elegantly seduce his wife who didn't need any enticing. (I think in any case she'd had enough and had probably wanted to engage in some kind of fisticuffs herself as her husband was such an arrogant prat).

The Selfridges intervention was also all about playing with consumerism in a kind of liberated way by taking apart its essential cash nexus and/or subverting the commodity form, in favour of plainly emphasising that everything has to be free. I guess this is why the intervention is still so powerfully remembered years later.

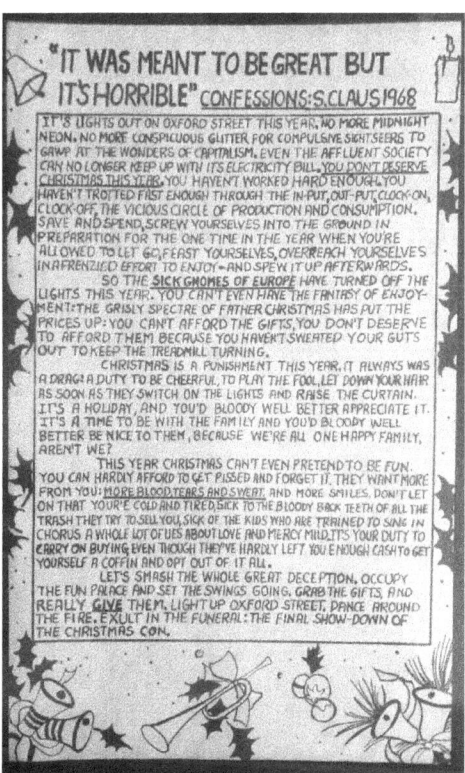

3 - THE 1970 SITUATIONIST REORIENTATION DEBATE

... and the 'Never Work'(ing) Workers...
Dave Wise
2011

This text describes a moment when the question was: were the 'workers', having lost the initiative of independent self-activity, becoming in the process reified beings and passive recipients of ideology the like of which we had never known? And yet hadn't Debord in his 1979 *Preface to the Italian edition of 'The Society of the Spectacle'* proclaimed 'to my knowledge it is the factories of Italy that this book has found for the moment its best readers.' Was this written in hope based on weaker facts or was something else taking place?

Certainly Debord's comments were well anchored as regards the wildcat strikes, constant sabotage and, especially amongst the protagonists, a growing 'lucid refusal of work and their contempt for the law and all Statist parties.' Therefore it seemed these workers were well prepared to subjectively grasp the wider ramifications and benefits from the best body of theory going.

It could be said that during the early 1970s there was a vague situ-like flavour to many workers' protests, thus the revolt against work in the 1970s started to figure high in a revamped ultra-left everywhere in Europe and America, which surfaced in many rightly acclaimed sizable publications from *Echange et Mouvement* in France, to John Zerzan's *Revolt Against Work* in America. However, it was never more than that; no conscious higher-level situationist disruption. That long wished for 'Strasbourg of the Factories' never really took place, though there were moments when small coteries of situationist-influenced workers had an effect in Italy, Spain and, briefly, among shipyard apprentices in Newcastle-upon-Tyne in England. (Possibly there were others that remain unknown).

The common denominator between all these separate forays was a 'lucid refusal of work' often playfully presented and very disruptive but never seeming to go beyond these promising beginnings which still remain hanging there tantalising us with curiosity; memories of what could have been if only protagonists had pushed harder, more creatively. Certainly those involved in these playful but deadly serious escapades never seem to have put reflective pen to paper so that we now would have had a better handle on things. Thus the disruption and communication remained largely on the level of the spontaneously verbal - typically a workers' reaction - perhaps like the realisation of free-form be-bop ensembles in their heyday but sadly, without the recording studio in tow! Only better!

In 1970 and post the uprisings of the late 1960s, a serious re-examination happened almost everywhere over a puzzling 'What do we do now' syndrome? More specifically in France there was *'The Orientation Debate within the Ex-Situationist International.'* This debate was basically in and around the limitations of past workers' councils. The debate had quickly concluded that a renewed similar explosively democratic body today would have to encompass a far wider critique of the totality of an ever-increasing alienated non-life. Debord specifically said, 'Its councils will have to be Situationist' with the demanding though lucid rider that, 'workers were going to have to come to the Situationists whilst remaining autonomous from what was left of the organisation'. In Debord's concomitant

'Problems of a Class Society' the crux of what's to come, 'demonstrates all the possible and desirable characteristics of the next revolution, analysing all the difficulties, serious uncertainties and the obscure points that it will have to overcome'. Note well here the emphasis on the obscure, because this was obviously a new tone; a possible new beginning and a warning about new pitfalls ahead.

The workers did not flock to Debord's salon as he so wished in the 'Reorientation Debate' (or somewhat demanded in that sub-Leninist disposition he often half-seriously donned, though with more than the flavour of a comic put-on, e.g. in the prelude to the founding manifesto of the SI in 1957 entitled *One Step Back*).There is much to be said still on this difficult conundrum. Yet so many thousands in the early 1970s avidly took bits and pieces of the best of situationist conclusions in basic active critique, renouncing all careerism but having no choice but to survive as part time workers. Only a few remained remorselessly carrying on with the quest.

At that time we and closest friends realised that those at the sharp end were going to have to go in for greater personal / social reflection; critiquing their own struggles more than ever, becoming dialecticians the more we were pushed up against the wall. Our published theoretical texts were therefore placed side by side with critical accounts by the combatants themselves, e.g. in *Wildcat Spain Encounters Democracy* via the way 'the workers' comments had been given profile in the magazines around *Contra a Corrente* in Portugal. A little later, in *France Goes off the Rail,* a largish pamphlet on the wave of French strikes in 1986, prominence was given to the detourned comics printed by the lascars; in short, apprentices appropriations of a situationist anti-publicity style. Sadly this development wasn't by any means advanced in the English speaking part of the globe though we were hoping these vital contributions would really begin to catch on in a future.. However in this have-assed / half-finished process many deep and drunken, lusty questions were thrown up which again must be prised open; otherwise only the museum of situationist texts and moments set in aspic will remain.

Previous to this development in the late 1950s / early 1960s, there had been recourse at the conclusion of Situationist conferences, for something like a quick snap shot of the workers, our friends, fraternising together! Well nice but what happens when push comes to shove? Around that time, or rather a few years after the *Reorientation Debate*, Jaime Semprum noted that some workers Debord had befriended on a relaxing pub level were a boring lot who weren't really saying much of interest. He may have been right; on the other hand that's how it is, though from the angle of 'the craic' (in the Irish sense of drift) is often how things germinate and then seemingly out of the blue, there's take-off. Certainly this warm, simple friendliness was at odds with the commanding tone of the theoretical / practical *Reorientation Debate*. Maybe Guy had sensed there was a problem here that needed to be more sensitively approached: weren't 'workers' with more than half an idea somewhat scared of approaching him wary of his ferocious reputation plus his considerable learning, anti-academic though it was? John Ruskin many decades previously after having published *Unto This Last*, a book much influenced by his sojourn in Bradford, was dismayed to learn that some workers in that quirkily clued-in though friendly city had wanted to meet him but were afraid to do so as they gad half-suspected he'd disparage them; an insult that would have been too dismaying in a life based on social rejection, made worse perhaps by Ruskin's final insistence in his book that that there is no other value in life than life itself.

One of the insulted and the injured named in *The Veritable Split*, a man who was regarded as a 'mediocre crook' regarding the theft of situationist funds, massively cast himself adrift and after a period of mental breakdown, slowly began to rebuild his life in an exemplary manner. His name is of course Rene Riesel and in the back of beyond on the Larzac plateau in south west France began to make an excellent subversive contribution; ironically working very hard as a renewed neo-peasant, massively deepening revolutionary eco-critique in an environment far removed from a world of too many artists, careerists, professional cop-out eco's, and cadres. Working hard for Riesel really did mean working hard, delightfully illustrated by a gal from *Os Cangaceiros* who a few years ago noted his bewilderment as a leather–clad, platoon-like, intellectualised, *Encyclopaedie des Nuisances* brigade with whom he was aligned, tried ineptly to build a makeshift market stall. Impatiently Riesel grabbed a hammer from them and did the job himself within a few ticks. (Ah, how well we understand that reaction!) As for Semprun, he went on to write some excellent stuff which shamefully hasn't been translated into English including *Abrege (A Brief Summary)* and a critique of Debord that isn't rancorous noting that, 'Debord is the last artist in a world without art'; thus intimating very perceptively that the next and last avant-gardes in pre-history will be the most persecuted of all as they will have no product to purvey or remotely commoditise. (In passing it should noted that in *Science & Capital* by the Dublin-based *Livewire Publications*, Phil Meyler – and ex King Mob – has recently translated some of Semprum's writings into English).

The 'dismal decade' of the 1970s was succeeded by something far more horrendous and which remains brutally impinging on us. The wildcat strike wave catastrophically collapsed especially in Europe and America wherever the neo-liberal free market was kicking-in and work, work, work, work, was to be acclaimed like never before. A 'new' worker appeared in the shape of 'presenteeism' ably abetted by a financial totalitarianism everybody at the sharp end was forced into submitting to. What remained of leisure (formerly free time) merely became an adjunct to work, often even more tiring and draining than 'work' itself. At the same time ever-increasing surveillance and the transformation of many workers forcibly press-ganged into acquiring auxiliary policing roles has meant all playful prospects and relaxation in everyday social space has been virtually extinguished. And all this is concomitant with the moment in south-east Asia a factory proletariat has grown up almost overnight and, larger than ever, is experiencing 19th century conditions of super-exploitation. It is in this contemporary chaotic nexus, on these disparate levels, that alienated non-life still must be broken apart.

4 - NIETZSCHE, WAGNER AND THE THEATRICALISATION OF MUSIC

Stewart Wise
2005

The following was sent to a young American woman putting together a re-appraisal of Black Mask and the Motherfuckers.

I am surprised Black Mask and the Motherfuckers are less well known in the States than King Mob and the French Situationists. Have you seen the recent book by Peter Doggett *There's a Riot Going On*, published by Canongate that deals with the 'revolution' in music, the title taken from Sly Stone's album of the same name? There are three pages on Black Mask and the Motherfuckers, in which the guy deals with the MC5 gig at New York's Fillmore East in which the Motherfuckers attacked hip entrepreneur Bill Graham. Although factually reasonably accurate, Doggett is essentially a musicologist living in Hampshire, England and he just hasn't a clue re wider, world-turned-upside-down perspectives, and manages to make historically important subversive incidents into very dull reading indeed. It's as though he can make no comment or take sides! The uniqueness of Black Mask/Motherfuckers was that they forthrightly attacked all the most advanced ultra-modern representations of capital and recuperations of real living, i.e. those aspects of general creativity emanating from those who wanted to live completely different lives. These representations included cultural mausoleums like the Rockefeller Center and Museum of Modern Art, hip police chiefs like Captain Fink, and 'cutting edge' pop musicians like Ed Sanders' Fugs and the MC5. It was a form of subversion unique in dissident 'other' America and has never been repeated there or its potential remotely fulfilled.

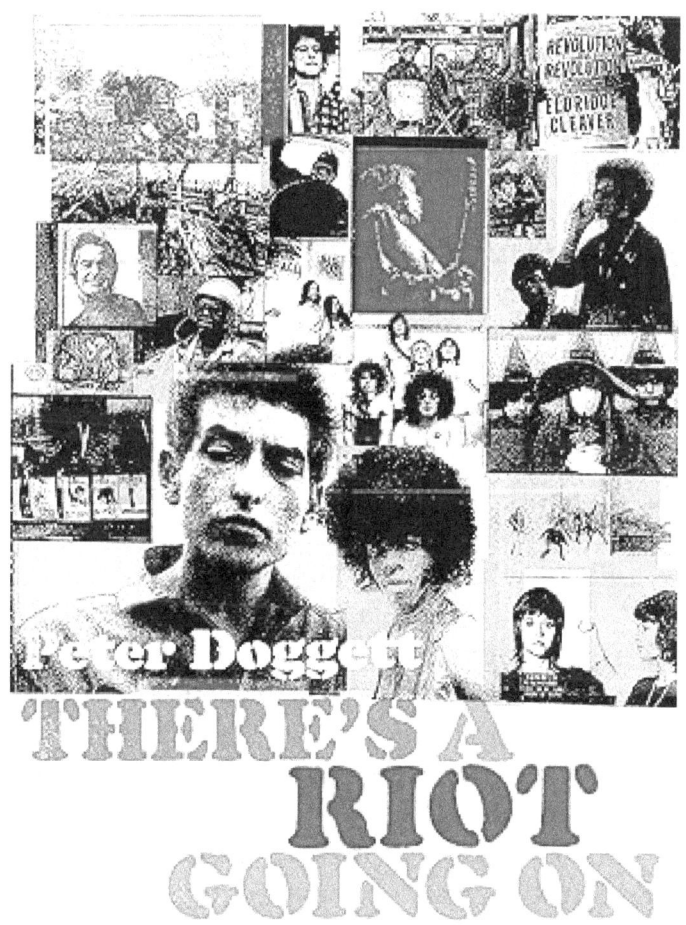

My brother David was involved in the Black Mask inspired

critique of Ed Sanders' record that became a hit with the lyric, 'art is nothing, nothing, nothing', which Dave saw as turning living contestation into an acceptable, saleable commodity. It must also be clearly understood that Ben Morea and Black Mask were the first to attack the role of pop music for its pivotal fulcrum in the vista of contemporary alienation. They were especially critical of the music that specifically said it was on the side of the revolution or indeed was the revolution itself. In reality it set itself against clued-in intervention from the street which could clearly go towards definitively overthrowing the audience/performer estrangement.

These facts in themselves also point to a wider historical memory or historical subconscious; as modern interventions like that outlined above didn't just come from nowhere.

So, apropos of music and your interest in Nietzsche, I am increasingly of the view the Nietzsche-contra-Wagner polemic is a seminal document of modern times and of massive importance as regards the present musical panorama; for that is what it is: a visual, wrap-around panorama of artistic enactments that endeavours to become all encompassing. The panorama strives, through the aid of the increasingly sophisticated minimalist gadgetry of quantum mechanics, to encompass all of life and eventually become a substitute for life (a 'second life' or 'skin' for quantum mechanics via computing; indeed, Craig Venter is on the verge of creating a replicant biology in tandem with implant engineering - compensating for the absence of the first).

Essentially, however, it has its (primitive) origins in Wagnerian stagecraft that aimed at a similar total immersion. Having its roots in the *gesamtkunstwerk* prefigured by German philosophical idealism, the importance it granted to art and the intuitive imagination was a parallel making of society which had to escape the confines of art to become a real force (though it was never stated quite as bluntly as this, all the elements are there that allow one to do so). It was also a response to the revolution of 1848 in some subtle, unremarked measure;

something which was never given the slightest credence by musicologists influenced by Bakunin and revolutionaries of the same ilk who for a short time Wagner befriended.

In place of *The Twilight of the Gods*, the *Gotterdammerung*, there arose the god of music as exclusively masterminded and choreographed by Wagner: the demiurge who Nietzsche denounced as being unable to save music and take his insight to the extremes it patently cries out for. As you probably know, the young Nietzsche idolised Wagner; he would embarrassingly abase himself in front of him and for several year was his step'n'fetch'it before turning on his idol with a vengeance, administering the most painful blow ever to land on him.

Nietzsche's first book, *The Birth of Tragedy,* brims with all the naïve verve of youth that was so effusive in praising Wagner. Guy Debord rated the book highly, and indeed, one can see how some of its concepts shaped Debord's theorising. It later became apparent that his aversion to Wagner became unbearable, though brilliantly obsessive, with Nietzsche worrying over every detail of Wagner's music, life and influence. In Nietzsche's eyes, Wagner could not do right for doing wrong.

Nietzsche refers to the Paris Commune of 1871 only as the 'Franco-Prussian War', unawares that this signal event in the history of class struggle had perhaps affected his profound enquiry into the nature of Greek drama and its codicil: the apotheosis of Wagner as a contemporary recreation of the spirit of Greek drama. Nietzsche by now was finding the auditorium and the company of performers/singers/actors – 'miming maniacs' - to be suffocating. Glad to be away from it all in the clean air of mountain passes humming with the sounds of insects he found a new innocence beyond the Judaic Christian morality that Wagner has become a declining and interminable prisoner of. This was not least because of his belief in total artistic envelopment as a panacea capable of possessing the power to cure the catastrophic alienation of man under capitalism. In so far as he once could accurately diagnose alienation, it has to be said that Wagner was closer to Marx than

Nietzsche ever was, though neither Marx or Engels could even begin to contemplate engaging on a critique of Wagner or even see it as essential. Here Nietzsche, as a reluctant 'communist' increasingly alive to the decay of artistic form, definitely had the drop on both of them.

In any case, the growing theatricalisation of music, the triumph of the means of production over performance goes back to Wagner, though no one, but no one, has the wit today to compare the Live Aid nonsense and Live Earth gore with the sound/performance orgies emanating from Bayreuth. Just consider the latter's obvious influence on the Nuremberg rallies and their gradual morphing into today's pop spectaculars with a penetration amounting to billions of viewers –something that Wagner and Hitler would have died for.

I also think it unfortunate that Nietzsche never had much to say about Hegel. Though describing him somewhere as a 'brother genius' (the other brother being Schopenhauer) I am inclined to think he had only cursorily dipped into Hegel; much preferring Kant. And it is Kant's philosophy that we see peering through the shades of *The Birth of Tragedy* time and again, particularly the importance Kant grants to the 'thing in itself' and the limitation such a concept imposes on scientific knowledge. As such, Nietzsche looks to destructive, galvanic 'creativity' as prefigured n the drunken Dionysian hordes, out of which Greek drama sprang and which is also a mythologisation of the Indo-European migration that, reading between Nietzsche's lines, posed the key question of quiescence - Buddhism - or action to provide meaning in preference to the knowing - and passive - distance of science.

I think it entirely false to claim that Nietzsche repudiated science and that his entire philosophy was a repudiation of reason (as for instance George Lukacs alleged) in the name of an altogether different epistemology ultimately derived from a defeated religion and renascent 'art' conceived as a principle of life. For instance, he followed with considerable interest Helmholtz's investigations into quicker–than-thought reflex actions and he was much taken with Nageli's researches into amoebal life forms, the latter in particular prompting thoughts on alimentation and the psychology of hunger that many years later were to knock Freud sideways. However, Nietzsche's claim that these amoebal forms show a rhythmic, aesthetic propensity goes well beyond Kant, even if Nietzsche's assertion that 'life can only be grasped as an aesthetic phenomena' is indebted to Kant, whilst clearly transgressing the restricted sense Kant grants to the aesthetic as alone being able to bridge the otherwise unbridgeable antinomy of pure and practical reason.

Rereading *The Genealogy of Morals* after a time span of thirty years I was particularly struck by the number of references to insects (there is a distinct buzz to the entire book) even going so far as to list the number of occasions insects are mentioned – and never unfavourably. To my mind it is an altogether less strained work than *Thus Spoke Zarathustra* (and that reflects Nietzsche's jealously as regards Christianity as he could never entirely overthrow the myth of the saviour). In *Zarathustra* biblical images of eagles and serpents abound (insects rarely appear in the bible other than negatively, like the plagues of locusts).

Nietzsche as an entomologist? Why, I even wrote a few lines on the subject several years ago with a eye to the founding fathers of modern entomology like Hooke, Leevanhoek, Ray and Schwammerdam, all four of whom were coincidental with the rise of Protestantism (described by Marx as "religion's self criticism") - and capitalism. In their work, insects are described as acting in various ways as living picture writing, and emphasis is placed on the astonishing formal variety of insect morphology and range of insect behaviours, thus implying a critique of the growing uniformity of life under capitalism. Although this admonition is far from obvious in the work of the aforementioned individuals, by the time Keats came to write his *Ode to Psyche* it certainly was.

To my mind Nietzsche in *The Genealogy of Morals,* and in other stray references throughout his oeuvre, had taken the subject a stage further by impishly, and perhaps involuntarily, linking entomology to a rejection of the past towards a rebirth of wonderment, innocence and a freedom from guilt. Nietzsche presents a nascent critique of political economy in the *Genealogy*, as is evident from the attention he pays to language, pointing in particular to the verb 'deber' meaning both to owe a sum of money and to do one's moral duty.

Need I say more? It certainly goes some way in helping elucidate the extraordinary hold entomology has over the me and my twin brother. And could the increased interest in insects we see appearing everywhere be a basis for a deeper, more larval, and yet soaring critique of capitalism which will help this downtrodden, desperately saddened humanity to eventually take wing and become inspired? Also, that Nietzsche was a proto-ecologist is never noticed. He arraigned industrial capitalism in the *Genealogy* for its hubris in full expectation of the nemesis to follow: 'Our whole attitude to nature, our violation of nature with the help of machines and the heedless ingenuity of technicians and engineers is hubris'. In the next breath he describes God as some putative spider, that spider taking the place of Kant's categorical imperative and forever weaving a web of deception in terms of final causes we must combat and which *is* our categorical imperative. This is the only time arthropods, as far as I can recall, are treated, if not in a wholly negative manner, then certainly ambiguously in the *Genealogy*. Otherwise to be in the presence of insects is an ennobling experience, and beyond good and evil, as these 'opposites' have hitherto been conceived. Nietzsche's final work, written when he was 'mad', correct me if I am mistaken, was *Ecce Homo.* To me it stinks of religious envy and to my mind it would have made more sense to have written a work entitled "Ecce Arte" - behold the artist or art. Its consequences could have been, would have been, far more profound – and relevant. Zarathustra sought to be a creator of life, of people, rather than art, but unfortunately he comes across as something of a crank prophet obsessed with replacing Christ, though he is unable to do much more than emulate what he was striving to overcome. And with nothing like the equivalent degree of success. In fact, when all is said and done Zarathustra is not much more than a ridiculously still born literary figure. Hegel also made Christ out to be an artist in his *Philosophy of the Fine Arts*, but Hegel, despite paying lip service to Christianity for career reasons, was a less religiously obsessed man than Nietzsche and his Christianity never detracted for one moment from his main task, which was to historicize the forms of art. This was a stupendously productive enterprise and which willy-nilly influenced Nietzsche and everyone else who subsequently has given a moment's thought to it.

5 - KURT SCHWITTERS' BARN: A TALE OF TWO CITIES

Dave Wise
2013

The *Schwitters in Britain* exhibition at Tate Britain (January to May 2013) features artefacts loaned out from the Hatton Gallery, Newcastle. The Hatton catalogued some technical sketches the Wises made in the mid-60s when doing a survey of Kurt Schwitters' Merzbau barn in the Lake District, supervised by Richard Hamilton for the purpose of rehousing it in the Newcastle gallery. The Wises' input was based on technical drawing learnt in the engineering classes of County Durham's secondary modern mining schools. Obviously, these technical supplements were little more than pieces of throwaway functional scrap paper and yet they've now become canonised as art.

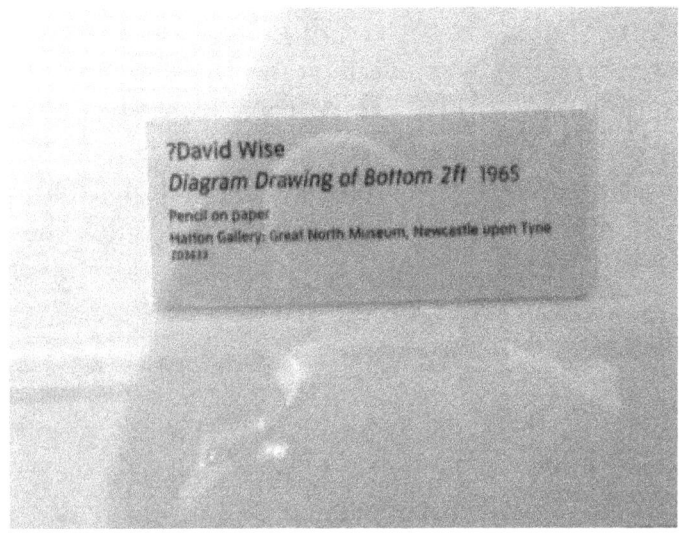

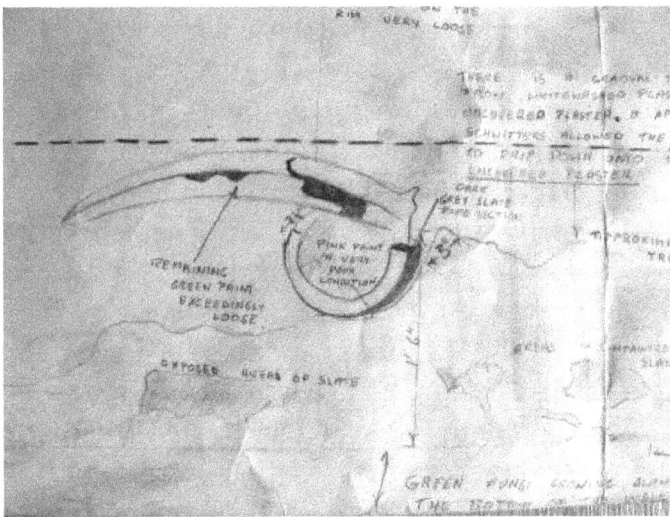

March 21st 2013 email to Nik Holliman
Dear Nik,
Our drawings in the Schwitters exhibit in Tate BritainRegarding the drawings in the Tate Gallery exhibition of Kurt Schwitters in early 2013 some funny business seems to have taken place. I was initially emailed by Gordon Moir in Newcastle in late 2011 saying he'd got a few drawings/photos of mine. Gordon who was in the Castoriadis-inclined Solidarity group was briefly a flat mate in Newcastle and I hadn't heard from him in decades.

Stuart wrote quite a longish thing on him in his Newcastle reminiscences which was available on the RAP web. Anyway, I was delighted to hear from him. Almost immediately there was an email from this guy called Rob Airey enclosing PDF copies of drawings attributed to me. I'd forgotten I'd done them but then clearly remembered I had. I then realised via a quick check on the Internet that this Rob Airey was curator of the Hatton Gallery in Newcastle. Anyway I then sent him a long email.

April 30th 2012,

Dear Rob Airey,

   Thanks for your email. Yes I did some drawings plus I took some photographs of Schwitters' Merz Barn as requested by Richard Hamilton, who recommended I do some of the initial work, knowing my interest in Dada. I think most of the drawings were connected with the cow bier location amidst the Lake District Fells though I'm not fully clear about this. My bro' (Stuart) may have done some drawings too as he cleaned the installation up together with Fred Brookes. I do remember I was initially very impressed with the outside of the relatively new barn – in comparison say to a Wordsworthian barn circa 1800 – when the farmer took us up the steep grassy path to it. As for the interior, well, I was initially struck by the smell of the cows which still occasionally inhabited the place and noted the patches of cow dung on the coloured, plaster relief looking so pleasantly dilapidated. Maybe sheep used the place too but it was the presence of the cows which particularly delighted me. (Incidentally there were no cows in the barn when Roger Westwood and I looked at it though there was plenty of trampled hay on the floor so perhaps sheep also used it or maybe it was simply a general over-wintering venue.) I know I did a quick sketch of a pretend cow next to the Schwitters simply to suggest the dung but whatever happened to that I just don't know.

   I distinctly remember I really liked the farmer as he was genial, voluble, clued-in and obviously really liked Kurt. Much later I couldn't help but reflect on the openness of the Lake District's 'peasant' locals, so responsive, so open-minded and therefore it came as no surprise to learn later that both Wordsworth and De Quincey married local gals. Obviously that splendid tradition was still continuing in the time of Kurt Schwitters simply because he didn't seem to have experienced any prejudiced anti-German sentiment, not forgetting this was during and just after the Second World War. He also could easily have been discriminated against as a dangerous eccentric and that seems never to have happened either.

I know I was very impressed with the location – still very vivid to me – so even at the time I thought it was wrong to move the Merz Barn to the dead space of a museum in Newcastle simply because of the co-incidental brilliant strangeness of its location. Obviously if the Merz Barn had stayed on the fells – and it is the best of all Schwitters Merz Barns largely because of the general environmental ambience – it would so easily have fitted in with the radical romantic early 19th century imagination; in fact an extension of that anti-artistic formal disposition in an unforeseen way. Its imprint on the Lake District would then have possibly been inseparable (if you like) from De Quincey's opium experiences say, in Grasmere churchyard and the birds he revived with his 'doddenum' (as his children called his laudanum), Coleridge's translations from the German of Kant's central thesis regarding the triumph of unadorned nature over artistic representation, plus perhaps Wordsworth's emphasis on the pre-surrealist, other worldly quality of the Lake District (especially the stillness) in comparison to the Swiss lakes; a comparison which Wordsworth emphasised somewhat. (Was this in his Notebooks?)

And then an interesting example of 'objective chance' took place (that coincidence which is perhaps more than coincidence and as extolled by Classical German Philosophy, the Surrealists, especially Breton and even later – and surprisingly – by Debord). The Schwitters affair took place in the mid 1960s and of course, Stuart helped considerably in the Merzbau reinstatement and lengthy conservation (matching up colours etc.) By then the short lived Icteric experiment was taking off and then after the fire and fury it provoked (together with early King Mob) I was more or less forced to leave Newcastle and went to London. I found a cheap bed sit in Notting Hill and to my surprise a little later I realised was exactly the house in St Stephens Crescent that Kurt Schwitters had lived in on the run from Nazi Germany.

It was in this place that Kurt conducted some gentle, amusing comments on English mannerisms e.g. 'When I am talking about the weather I know what I'm talking about' etc. and the character of "Wantee" was invented obviously based on the endearingly friendly cockney woman who was always asking Kurt 'Would you like a cup of tea'. I am sure the same person was still there in the late 1960s as an old dear in this friendly down home house was always asking me if I'd like some tea!

Anyway I digress. I don't know if these notes will be useful.
Best: Dave Wise
I DIDN'T HEAR ANYTHING MORE FROM EITHER OF THEM.
I was rather surprised as both replies from me were pleasant enough even when writing to such an arsehole as a curator. Then I heard of the Schwitters exhibition and began to put two and two together. It would appear I'd been hoodwinked and I suspect money was involved and for some reason I wasn't informed. Alas it seems to be part of that old Newcastle trajectory - so here I am again regarded as the same old piece of shit – treated with disdain and not worthy of being levelled with. Initially I had to get away from Newcastle in the late 1960s because I was on a blacklist and the police were in hot pursuit. But what's going down now? Simple: snide rubbishing and perhaps a rip-off? After all, I'd specifically told the art establishment they were my technical drawings; so why the peculiar question mark before my name in the Tate? What are they trying to hide? Also I noticed Stuart's name wasn't mentioned even though he had more to do with the Schwitters Merz barn than I did! Plus ca change. Best Dave (later Nik was to send a letter to the Tate Gallery pointing a few things out)

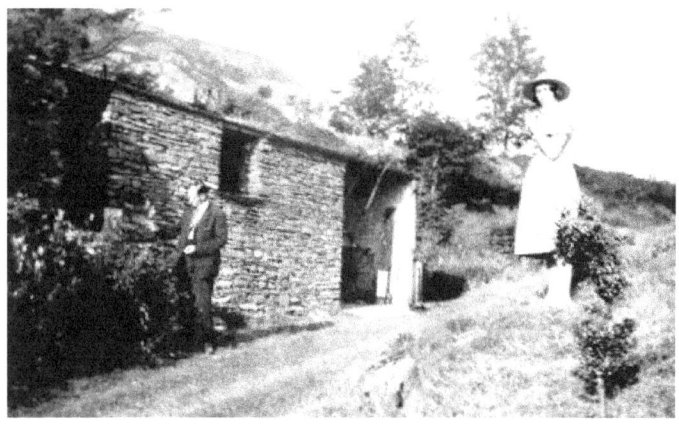

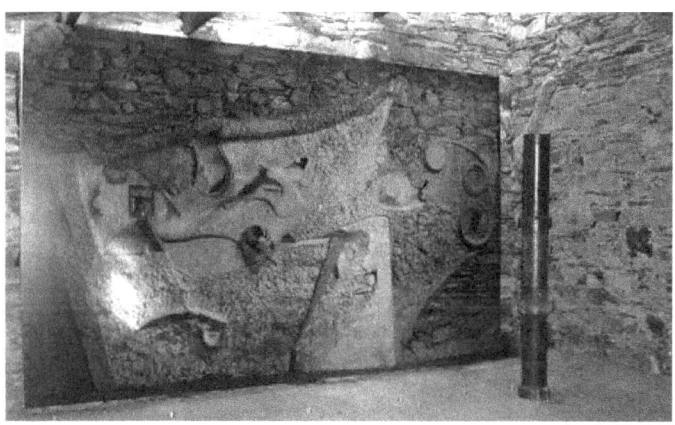

Obviously these technical supplements were little more than pieces of throwaway functional scrap paper and yet they've now become canonised as art. As a friend said apropos the drawings, 'Is there nothing un-sacred'. That some of Kurt Schwitters' connectedness with the Lake District should have rubbed off on the brief moment that was *Icteric* in Newcastle from 1966 to the summer of 1967, is hardly surprising. It did have an indirect influence on a mocking, primitivist, marquette we constructed and positioned out in the wilds of Northumberland. We photographed these blush making efforts and sent the prints off the Dick Higgins of the *Something Else Press* in New York with a view to them being published in a book he was preparing on 'fantastic architecture'. (We have gone into this slightly embarrassing episode elsewhere so there is no point in repeating it here.) Apart from anything else, we were mindful that Huelsenbeck had considered Schwitters a petite bourgeois and not of the same calibre as other German Dadaists like Johnny Heartfield, George Grosz, and especially Franz Jung and Johannes Baader The latter two engaged in daredevil, highly imaginative interventions, despite Jung harbouring Bolshevik illusions. Baader would eventually be banged up more or less permanently in psychiatric institutions, and which might well have saved him from certain death in Hitler's concentration camps.

What provoked Huelsenbeck's ire in particular was the fact that Schwitters was a landlord in 1930s Hamburg and had evicted a tenant so he could extend his Merzbau upstairs onto the first floor. In our naïve, though probing way, we were reliving vital perceptions handed down to us from the past; a past that could all of a sudden come alive and the revolutionary project resumed as if preserved in aspic. So we were delighted to learn through an ex *Os Cangaceiros* guy exiled in Berlin that in the early 1990s Johannes Baader, amazingly still alive and kicking, was still the commendable madman of old. He had responded to the fall of the Berlin Wall like it was 1919 all over again and the German Revolution in full swing. He had journeyed around Berlin sticking up posters that read in big letters, ALL POWER TO THE WORKERS' COUNCILS. Jeez, we couldn't help but be impressed despite our conviction that to try imposing the original councilist project on today's society was plain bats because it failed to recognise the socially destructive, ecologically toxic nature, of most work and production.

And then we found something even more necrotic that once more brought Icteric and Schwitters into an opaque proximity that was at once apparent to us but to very few others. The installation artist in question is one Laure Prouvost, a contender for the Turner Prize who had a video installation running throughout the Tate Britain 2013 Schwitters exhibition. In this pointless video she invents a relationship between herself and Schwitters. In other pieces, the influence of Icteric is obvious; Prouvost revamping motifs without, it goes without saying, acknowledging their origins. In a typical karaoke performance one sings along to an acknowledged original. However the kind of karaoke practised by Prouvost postures as the original whilst the original begetters sink into oblivion; their names never to be mentioned on the public stage. The heist is perfected when the copy becomes the original, the shyster becomes the honest broker and stealing becomes restitution. Let the prize money roll in tribute to this turning upside down!

In a recent exhibition at the Whitechapel art gallery Ms Prouvost exhibited a shoe with a legend posted above that read 'this is the shoe found being carried by hundreds of butterflies from Italy to Central London on the day of St Buitano'. In a video clip butterflies were seen 'puddling' on the same shoe which, if not deliberately staged for the camcorder, had doubtless congregated there to sup up the nitrate- rich human sweat. (See *As Common as Muck* in our book, *Dialectical Butterflies*). Elsewhere there's an obviously staged film clip of fish with strawberries in their mouths and there's even a photo of a slug with the word 'Lux' in the corner (Lux evidently is some wanky avant-garde film/image collective).

All these images have their origins in the Icteric experiment, even down to the references to none existent saint. At that time Trevor Winkfield of Icteric was way ahead of the pack in introducing Eric Satie to an uncomprehending English speaking world, creating the piss-take esoteric cult of 'Saver of Souls of the Metropolitan Church of Art of Jesus, Foreman'. From his bed sit 'abbey' Satie would excommunicate people and issue edicts, whilst concurrently weighing notes, the forerunner of the endless loop and never-ending performance, generally taking music apart at the seams, beginning with the ditching of barlines. Satie would also eventually join the Communist Party – indeed was even on the party's central committee whilst dressing as a 'bourgeois functionary'. Maybe it could be said that

Satie would have been better off with the anarchists but there again, in terms of total critique were the anarchists that much better at the time? For certain Satie was stumbling towards greater coherence but his was also a world in flux, just as the mid 'sixties were beginning and anything seemed possible..

Laure Prouvost won the 2011 Max Mora prize for women artists, which included a six month residency in Italy to produce work for exhibition in London's Whitechapel Art Gallery in 2013. The Max Mora prize says much about the changing status of women and glass-ceiling feminism. Max Mora is an Italian fashion house, and from its founding in 1950 was opposed to the aristocratic ethos surrounding haute couture. Its rise to becoming an international company parallels the rise of contemporary feminism, only really taking off in the 1970s. It aimed to produce designer, easy-to-wear clothes in luxury fabrics for the 'new woman' market, i.e. the woman who has turned her back on traditional roles but is not in revolt against capitalism, so in fact appears to be able to take it or leave it like a Max Mora fashion garment. The firm's director stressed, 'our customers are led by fashion but are never its slaves'. Laure Prouvost fits that bill to perfection.

Ms Prouvost also worked as an assistant to the late auto-destructive artist, John Latham, who, of course, was familiar with Icteric; continuing to praise the experiment whilst we increasingly grew ashamed of it. Right up to the end, Latham remained stuck in the same groove, becoming, after an initial flurry that got him the sack from St Martin's School of Art, a tiresomely repetitive, bogus anti-establishment figure whose house front in south London was made over to resemble two giant books, their intertwined pages emerging from the facade.

In 1966, Latham formed the Art Placement Group (APG), which aimed to position avant-garde artists in industry thus, in principle, enabling them to play a central role in production, which he thought would result in a more imaginatively driven capitalism. This half baked idea, originating in the continental Fluxus group, would have rightly been laughed to scorn and dismissed out of hand by the Situationists. When a radical critique finally did break in this country, and Latham found himself in the firing line, it lasted all of ten. His avant-garde update of Olde Englande gets ever more 'olde' with each passing year, eventually sweeping all before it.

Meanwhile, from 1975 to '76, Latham would be employed by the Scottish Office's Development Agency to come up with ideas about what to do with 19 massive shale heaps in Lothian, left behind by an industry that used to extract oil from the shale that would then be turned into paraffin. Latham, not surprisingly, immediately acknowledged their beauty and argued that they be left as they were and be designated monuments. Or rather, not quite as they were; the innately 'superior' perception of the artist changing them into 'process sculptures', a piece of elitist fanny that even the Scottish Development Agency would endorse when its chief planner said .the product is not an art work but a report by the artist on new ways of looking at chosen work areas.

Though we literally gag at the thought of ever calling ourselves artists, we are slowly coming to the conclusion that to charge anti-eco, greenwash opponents with cultural philistinism is the most potent weapon in our armoury; especially where it concerns the destruction of nature-rich brownfield sites. An inventory of wild life species that will be destroyed is of little consequence besides that of a wide ranging knowledge of the cultural avant-garde of the 20th century and its continuing fall-out. The fact that Latham's 'process' sculpture remains a keystone to the preservation of other threatened 'bings' (businesses want to use the valuable shale for building material) is something we can learn from and cynically use if it helps achieve our conservationist aims and does not require we surrender our principled opposition to the likes of Latham and similar artistic coteries.

Latham would remain a prisoner of passive aesthetics, of the viewer with bad eyesight and no hands, of money, fame, flattery…and female studio assistants. That said the APG did want to materially engage with industry (though certainly not with capitalism) and was therefore a tad different to today's satiety of artists in residence who generally tend toward much more traditional conceptions of art. Latham once had the makings of a mover and shaker, but in the end his life is a squandered life. And perhaps that is source of his appeal to those who also betrayed their better selves; such as the equally ridiculous ex-King Mobber, Phil Cohen, who still finds Latham's crap challenging and has recently been promoing it alongside other, even more conventional, shit buttressed with quotes from postmodernist arseholes like Derrida. In fact Phil Cohen is one of the by now sizable army of bedraggled 'returnees' mimicking late-1960s radicalism minus the essential cutting edge and covering up all the shit they've been involved over the last 35 years or so. As a respectable professor he once not so long ago thought Thatcherism was inevitable, striking miners quite ridiculous and we in the UK in desperate need of a new Winston Churchill. Mysteriously all that has now been air brushed from history as the new fad of 'radicalism' is proclaimed.

Most of the above information revolves around sub-artistic rip-off in one way or another, so perhaps it's worthwhile mentioning a liberating crime we committed in those far-off days. One dark night as Icteric was morphing into direct action and its 'members' becoming more aggressive, a number of us broke into Richard Hamilton's Newcastle studio and nicked a number of his things, more as trophies than anything else. Really there wasn't much there but we did purloin a couple of his old etching plates. later putting them between the heavy rollers of an old lithographic press producing passable black and white reproductions. We did it for the cheek of it without thought of pecuniary gain as none of us were into money-making in any serious way. In big trouble with authorities and in flight from Newcastle as the 1960s ended, we left much of our gear behind. It seems the etching printouts were taken by our elder brothers who had aggressively turned against us, horrified by our opinions and actions, especially our anti-art activities, and turning us over to the forces of an increasingly nasty reaction in its many disguises. Ever after we had little or nothing to do with them until their deaths as we couldn't forgive their intensifying philistinism. We now find through the Internet that these etchings have been sold off for nigh on twenty grand! So in no way were we ever to be in receipt of the proceeds of a 'crime' that wasn't about money in the first place; for indeed our 'crime' was about something else entirely: more an add-on to our anti art activities. As for criminals we would suggest a different interpretation or, as a friend said of us recently, 'strange, intense, criminal agitators of the heart' - a comment he picked up from Kerouac's *Big Sur*. We were more than flattered...

6 - MALEVICH IN THE 21ST CENTURY

The Square as Recuperation

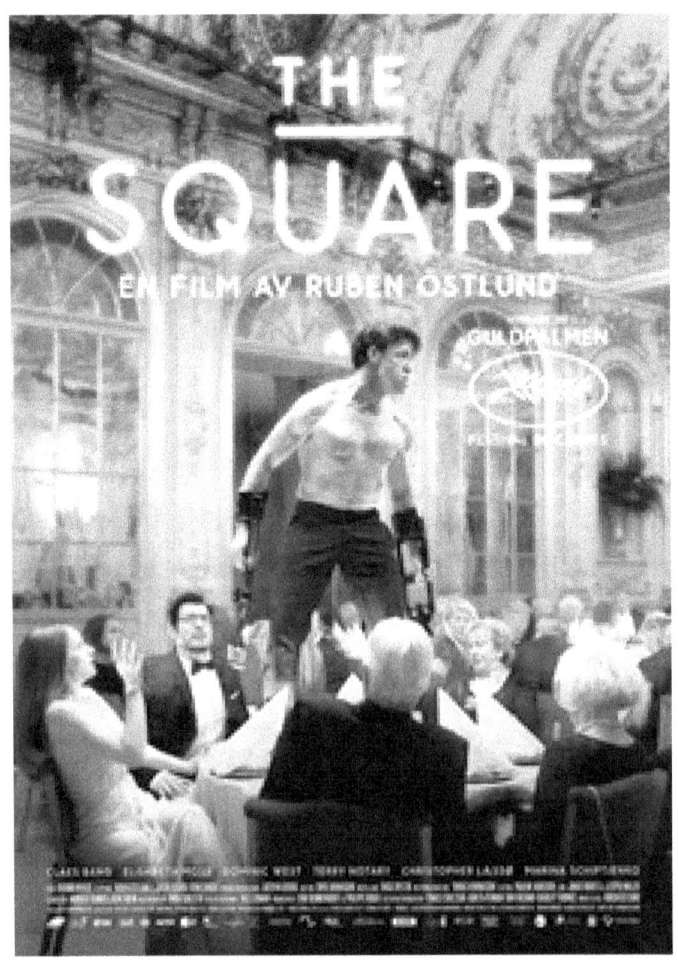

KING MOB: THE NEGATION AND TRANSCENDENCE OF ART

Dave Wise
2019

The Square, a film released in 2017, was written and directed by Ruben Östlund. A Swedish production with co-production support from Germany, France and Denmark, it won the Palme d'Or prize and was nominated for the Academy Award for Best Foreign Language Film at the 90th Academy Awards.

Commenting onthe real origin of *The Square* takes us back to the 1960s and our involvement in an authentic anti-capitalist cum anti-art movement back in Newcastle-Upon-Tyne. Needless to say, in this there was creative investigation and contestation together with the inevitable fuck-ups. Subsequently, it wasn't superseded but derailed, through a stealthy - even lethal - banal recuperation. Almost immediately a step backwards was taken as the contestation was frozen into a museum exhibit that became something of an iconic big hit in the world of what is acceptable. This was T*he Poetry Will be Made by All! Transform the World* exhibition put together by Ron Hunt from Newcastle, and curated by Pontus Hulten in Stockholm's Moderna Museet in 1969. The exhibit combined neglected moments from Russian Futurism with a big emphasis on Malevich's Suprematism, along with montages put together by Stuart Wise illustrating Surrealist ideas for the transformation of Paris in the 1930s. The exhibition also featured various incendiary images and manifestos from the here and now, especially from our then collaborators, New York's Black Mask and Motherfuckers.

This was the moment, however, when authentic revolt world-wide was beginning to stagger out of the shadows, unsure of what to do and where to go next. In its turn the Moderna Museet exhibition sparked numerous acts of what quickly morphed into tried and trusted pseudo-confrontation, safely ensconced within the recently updated paradigms of an art world where everything 'changed' in order to remain the same.

(Examples of this so-called change was the rise of performance art. which transformed into the 'land art' movement of Robert

Smithson, Andy Goldsworthy and Richard Long, etc - secondary imitations of authentic contestation which managed to look original because of its new eco edge, which preceded the descriptive *greenwash* definition,).

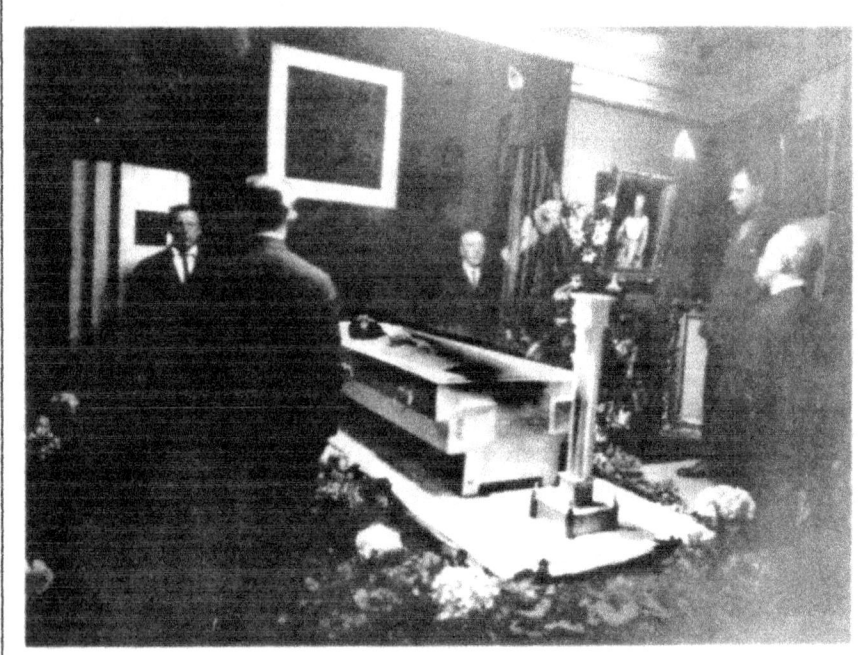

Kasimir Malevich's funeral, Leningrad, 25th of May 1935

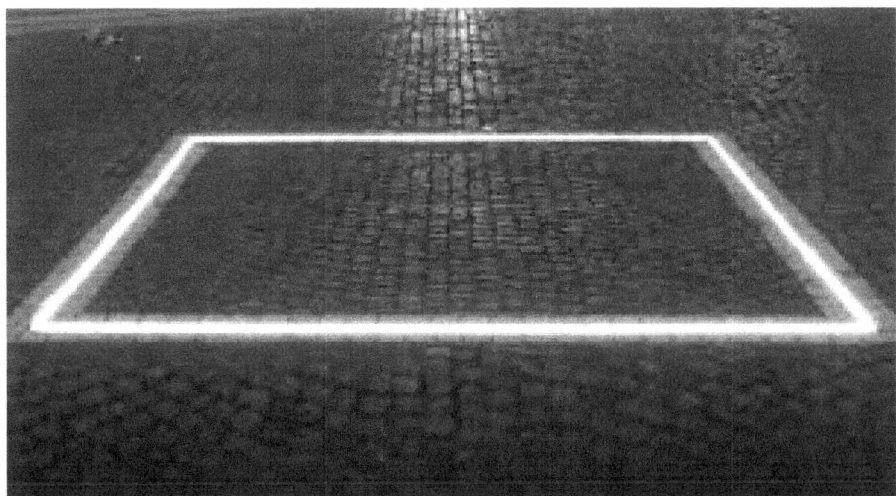

The neon-lit 'white' edge of the Black Square from the 2018 film

Alas, decades of stasis were to pass before the original **Moderna Museet** exhibition of 1969 was again recognised as an 'iconic' moment which needed to be somewhat remembered / repeated / celebrated again. Thus a fallout organisation from the German performance art 'Happeners' Fluxus transformed into *e-flux* in January 2014, now presided over by Hans Ulbricht Obrist. A revamped, hipster-oriented curator, Obrist even interviewed authentic rebels like ex-situationist Raoul Vaneigem. Obrist had also taken over a top administrative position running Hyde Park's Serpentine Gallery in London along with other prestigious positions. *e-flux* was shortly followed with Obrist's ***89plus*** 2015 exhibition in both Zurich and, again, in Stockholm's Moderna Museet. Some of the promotional blurb for gallery did minimally tell the truth: 'The exhibition itself was inspired by the seminal 1969 show at the Moderna Museet'.

Immediately, the new repeat exhibit ricocheted. Deputy leader of the Corbynista Labour Party, John McDonnell MP; took it up, imitating the title and helping create the Momentum movement. By then ***89plus*** was a MSM /social media hit and in this air-conditioned maelstrom a film beckoned; one which would crown all previous endeavours. It found its raison d'être in *The Square,* which then went on to capture the establishment's top prize: the fekkin' Palm D'Or!

Strange, yet not strange at all, no doubt we will be accused of living on Fantasy Island, or if not that, simply being downright liars. But that's exactly how an elongated recuperation works, even as it becomes more far-fetched, even phantasmagorical. This particular event concerns cinema as the very axis of what was once lived passionately, turning into prize-winning, ultra-passive representation and resignation.

Is it unique? Not at all, as indeed something similar had happened over sixty years ago in France. Back to 1961 and the Cannes Film Festival. A certain 'notorious' Alain Resnais had just won the Golden Globe prize for his nouvelle vague French film *Last Year at Marienbad* based on an anti-novel novel by Robbe Grillet. Why notorious? Well, Resnais had been refused entry to the Cannes Film Festival because he had signed Jean Paul Sartre's manifesto of the 121 against the French Algerian war. At the time our miniscule authentic band of late-teen miscreants in Newcastle-Upon-Tyne didn't know about any of this until a year later when we piled into a tiny 'art' cinema on Northumberland Street, Newcastle's main drag. After having been recently turned-on at the same gaff by *Quatre Cent Coups* by Francois Truffaut we thought we couldn't go wrong. Uh-Huh. Walking out at the end one of us (David Young) said: "*Last Year at Marienbad*, bad, bad, bad". But we were young – and naive in another way - and though able to recognise Surrealist quotes and the Magritte-like cum De Chirico-like estrangement, we missed the essential: that this film was the recuperation of Lettrism. The latter's negation of cinema, with subversive concepts newly appeared as flippant and whimsical.

True, by 1961 we had heard of Lettrism, but basically knew nothing about its broad, perceptive theory and we certainly didn't know who Isidore Isou, the Lettriste 'leader' was. Nay, farther back, in deepest County Durham, a vague knowledge of the word Lettrism alongside skiffle had come to our attention in a loser's bottom-end secondary modern school on Kirk Merrington's pit spoil heap football field where we played the tough pit-laddies from the nearby pit villages of Pity Me and Seldom Seen. But back then there were no more salient subversive facts immediately blowing in the wind…

True, by 1961 we'd become more sophisticated but the *essential* was still missing: we didn't know about Guy Debord and his ground-breaking anti-film of 1952, *Howls in Favour of De Sade* made the very year the Lettrist International came into existence, having moved a step forward from Isou's more narrowly focussed Lettrism. And the crux of this 'film' - that no film was now possible, that cinema was dead - was dynamite. Henceforth – it suggested - shit on this passive contemplation of nothingness, this endless staring at a blank screen pointing towards a horrific empty visual world of things; of endless saleable commodities via a substitute life of spectacle. For sure, we knew something (though basically nothing) about *Howls in Favour of De Sade,* except that Allen Ginsburg's seminal Beat Generation eruption in America was a poem named *Howl.* We only realised the connection and its cultural recuperation via 'edgy' poetry some 10 years later.

Yes, we knew about avant-garde cinema but it was Eisenstein and Dziga Vertov that captivated and then on a more thrilling level, *A Propos de Nice / Zero de Conduite* by Jean Vigo followed by Rene Clair's *Entracte*, etc, but then – more explosively – there was Luis Bunuel's, *Le Chien Andalou* and *L'Age D'Or.* In comparison the more recent international recognition of the French nouvelle vague seemed tame in comparison. For sure we knew about the Cannes film festival and the opportunist antics of sometime surrealist Jean Cocteau who supported Hitler during the Occupation. We knew about Andre Breton, and despised him, though again we were lacking on essential details. We didn't know that in 1955 Cocteau had redesigned the Palme D'Or and that Isou had disrupted the official jury system appointing his own awards showing his film manifesto *"Treatise on Venom and Eternity"* outside the official grounds where 'A sizable commando of some thirty lettrists, all wearing the filthy uniform as their only really original trade mark, showed up at Cannes determined to provoke a scandal that would draw attention to themselves'.

This indeed was the post-Second World War rootless generation of vagrant rebels against work, refusing to market anything they produced such as their free Potlach mag The 'cadres' of Debord's new Lettrist Internationalbrought into being the ambience of an undomesticated derive and psychogeography. That year there were such ructions in Cannes that ever after the Palme D'Or became a pretty rigid event…..

In late 2017/early 2018, we contributed an article to Issue No.2 of *A VOID* magazine (published by Morbid Books), entitled 'Welcome to Future Ecocide'. In this, we weren't just offering another simplistic 'revolutionary' ecology in the sense of Murray Bookchin's statement that 'Ecology is the only revolutionary science'. We also invoked wider memories of past nature-oriented experiments around *Icteric* magazine in Newcastle in the mid to late 1960s; if you like, for the reshaping of humanity and nature inextricably combined.

To take a specific example: *Icteric* was also about the lost history of the Russian avant-garde at the time of the Russian Revolution and its immediate aftermath. The seminal figure of Malevich played a big part here, and we were duly fascinated not only with *White on White* and the *Black Square* but also Malevich's Suprematist coffin which we reconstructed together with a week-long performance art ritual, ending with one of us kicking to bits a replica painting of *The Black Square*.

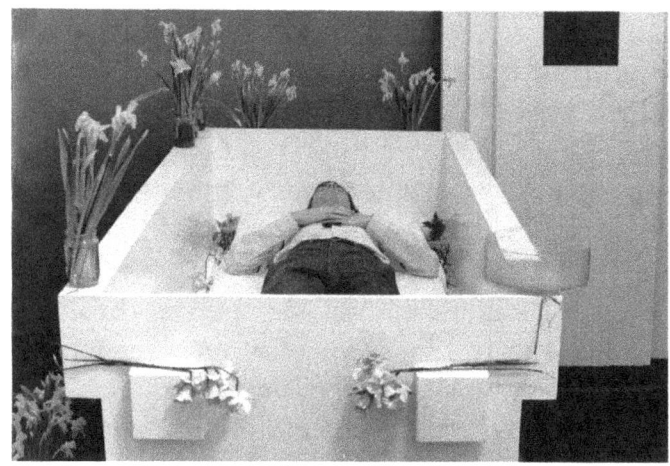

Naive yes, but we were basically fascinated by the tabla rasa Malevich announced as we ineluctably, two years later, became much more fascinated by Malevich's comments than his artefacts. We saw comments such as 'Come comrades, swim with us into the whiteness' as a prelude to prising open 'anarchy's new dawns' (perhaps more telling was Anton Ciliga's comment, written many years after Malevich's death, that the aura of Russia generally was 'despotism tinged with anarchy').

However, by then we had gorged on the forbidden fruit of the Situationists and, more knowingly, could then situate Malevich as an interesting stepping stone en route to a much more profound critique of art and culture in relation to capitalism, a critique which was – and still is – much more explosive. Sadly, we then noted that Malevich in his final years -- obviously feeling the full force of Stalin's despotism – was lapsing into really old time, cornball art products, such as self- portraits, etc.

The die was cast and from then on an increasing fascination with the failure of the Russian Revolution and European revolutions in general took over. But, the somewhat obsessive Russian puzzle won't go away just like that, especially that emphasis on active nihilist extremism. Would it break out again, and how?

We aren't about to go into the plot and narrative of *The Square* as anybody can read about that via the Wikipedia blurb or buy the DVD for a few quid. In any case that's of no importance here. This polemic is about establishing subversive markers that have been deliberately derailed to make an acceptable cinematic presentation.... Broadly, the film is supposed to be a comedy taking a gentlemanly piss out of performance art. Yawn, Yawn, Yawn ...

Right from the very beginning the *Icteric*-like gallery style spoil heaps appear and they keep on re-appearing throughout the 3 hour long film, except that in our present greenwash age they seem to alternate between piles of grain and piles of muck and sand. Re the latter, Robert Smithson is mentioned for his design, which plays on the real landscape/art installation rubbish, which has nothing to do with real ecological intervention within nature. And then, in the film perhaps a modern state-of-the-art vacuum cleaner accidently hoovers everything up. Laugh, Laugh, Laugh.... Ugh, Ugh, Ugh!

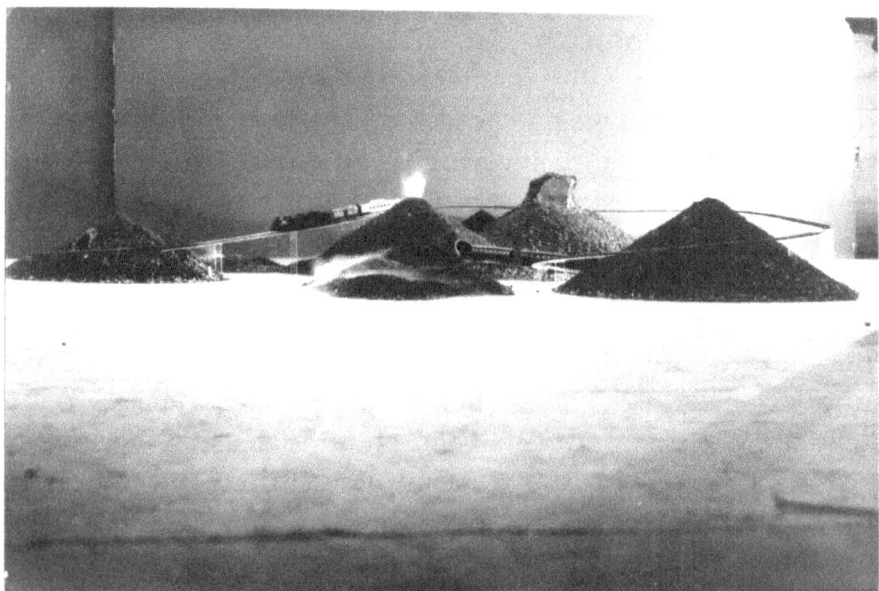

Above: Icteric spoil heaps on an art school floor in Newcastle

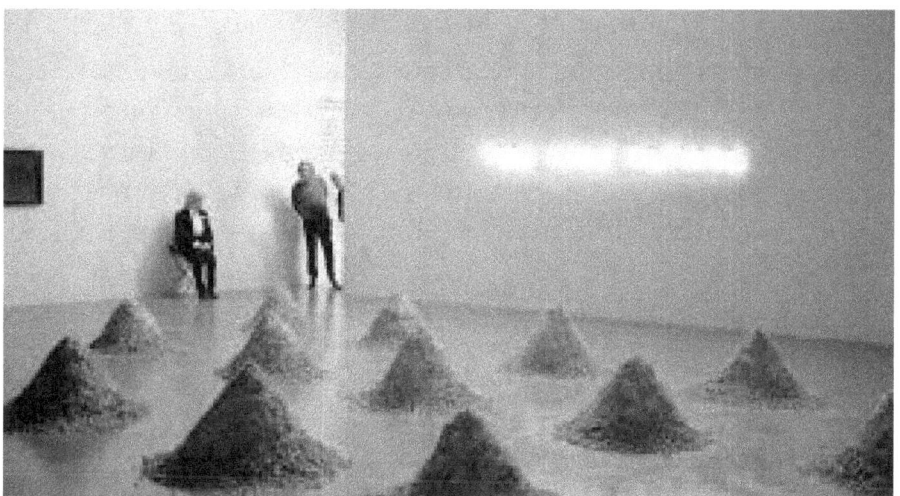

Above: The spoil heaps in the Palme D'Or film

Right from the very beginning too, the film is about the Stockholm based Museum of Modern Art getting into 'cutting edge art' on the level of Exhibition/Non-Exhibition, Site/Non-site. More specifically, it's about placing random objects in museum space where they are instantly re-anointed as art. In the film an old formalised bronze sculpted statue on a plinth of – most likely – some historically famous Swedish warrior on a horse is unceremoniously pulled off by a crane creating a new space for... a square. It quickly becomes obvious that this new square is based on Malevich's Black Square – though doesn't specifically say so - with its original white border replaced with a thin strip of white neon lighting (see above photo). In fact a much, much bigger new Black Square of 4 by 4 metres is cut into old cobblestones, replete with brass plaque proclaiming intentions: 'Equal rights and obligations'; 'The square is a zone of trust and care', etc, meant to 'activate the audience'.

Elsewhere, the film bangs on about 'relational aesthetics'. a combination of art and sociology. The film continually plays with provocative contestation from an anonymous audience activated and pissed-off with art language mumbo jumbo; only to be dismissed by the platform as a rash of tourettes syndrome when somebody calls the art 'garbage'. All pointlessly in-joke clever, clever bullshit.

Yet the backdrop is all ultra-modern, and is about the niche; the culturally-oriented *really* rich along with endless hi-tech gadgetry and Youtube videos. In short there's hardly any difference between the rich, disoriented, somewhat alienated bo-ho *La Dolce Vita* milieu of *Last Year at Marienbad* and the fuks portrayed here. So nothing much has changed in this respect. The original Lettriste milieu were more or less poverty stricken scruffs and we up north in 1960s England were hardly much different, making do in a real communal piss-up with home brew wine and beer. Cars figure in *The Square* narrative but the vehicle driven by the central caste bo-hos of course has to be a Tesla, manufactured by Elon Musk, an obnoxious multi-billionaire showman 'visionary' – who else? As for the art/anti art conundrum, it is only about one thing only: Big Money, boosted somewhat by the uninspiring 'creative' food obsession typical of affluent modern art museum audiences. In itself, in any case, the 'art' is about nothing more than finding the best piece of sensationalism going, one which will attract both the MSM and social media.

In short, in the gateway to Big Bucks a Malevich suprematist painting went for $60 million in a Sotheby's auction in New York in 2008. In the film the curators are the real subject, as they are the lynch pin of art valorisation; and in the film they hit the jackpot through a purposefully distasteful vid showing a poor kid blown apart within the space of the cobblestone square. Finally there's a pseudo-passionate appeal –seemingly spontaneous - for the ultra rich to put everything right in the world. Obviously there's nothing about obliterating the rich bastards once and for all.

Towards the end of the film its bye, bye *Icteric*, enter *King Mob* and the gorilla /donkey invasion of Powis Square, Notting Hill in 1968. In the film, a sedate, rich, cultured, gathering in a super de luxe luxury dining venue needs some frisson initiated by the organizers in a 'Welcome to the Jungle' episode. A guy imitating a gorilla enters and slightly fuks them around until he really

does get out of hand and then has to be knocked out cold by some now agitated members of the audience. In no way though does this episode subvert the audience/performer nexus central to the function of capitalism. Indeed, if anything the film is a paean of praise for the wonders of capitalism.
The camera pans over myriad ascending stairwells in a modernist block of high rise apartments for the poor. It's also a straight lift from a photo in our book, *Wildcat Spain Encounters Democracy,* entitled 'lean over the staircase we are going to hold an assembly'. None of this is about subversion and social revolution. This is about getting the highest shittiest monetised award in the film industry: the Palme d'Or at the Cannes film Festival plus the Goya award for best European film plus the Robert Award for best Non-American film…….and no doubt the the "plus" goes on and on and on ……

At the end of the film the credits contain a long, long, list of *all* those involved, that is apart from the initial **very real instigators** …. Always remember, only substitutes and pastiches are of any significance in an empty, ultra-commoditised, performance oriented society…

Of course there are no abominable copyright restrictions to anything we do and anybody is free to do whatever they wish. However, *The Square* steals in a predatory ultra-monetised way, not so 'ideas can be improved and plagiarism implies it' – mentioning yet again that great quote from Lautreamont – but so that real intervention can be further trashed and the real thought of history further derailed.

Then there's that other great axiom: 'Poetry will be made by all and not by one' though today even here we have now to add a big 'Yer-Wat?' Yeah, for sure the great slogan is from Isodore Ducasse's *Poesies* and not *The Songs of Maldoror* (remember that Ducasse wrote under the pseudonym of the Comte de Lautreamont – a posh title most likely imitating the example of Lord Byron – and a pseudonym which Andre Breton described as 'execrable'. Yep this axiom, along with so much else truly was a subversive lashing out that promised so much and yet today has got so lost, elongated, bent, and estranged; without, however, disturbing this baneful olde worlde with its endless facelifts. A world indeed that has bent over backwards to fully bring it on board without disturbing the status quo of art galleries / poetry gatherings / salons / lecture theatres / universities / cultural festivals / etc, and *essentially* the big dollario that *always but always* is present in these vacuous commoditised gatherings. For sure poetry will be made by all BUT as it stands in the dismal perspectives of these nastily reactionary times, is and will forever be *qua* poetry, *qua* painting, *qua* sculpture, qua music, *qua* architecture – all redundant cultural specialities - until we all throw up. Today an endless mediocrity gets ever worse as a smoke and mirrors increasingly valueless and as an unsubstantial capitalism heads at breakneck speed towards disaster, which yet in mundane day-to-day space and time, appears so unbearably slow in happening.

Finally, it's not as though our experience is unique. The film *The Square* mirrors to some extent, although in a much more camouflaged way, the story of the Monkey Wrench Gang in the America of the 1970s first transformed into a novel by Edward Abbey (and for a least the last 10 years has been proposed as the basis for a film starring Hollywood celebrities).

Way before that, in 1960, there was *The Train* which in turn inspired the German happener Wolf Vostell to re-enact in real life, the film's train crash when in reality the film was a kind of Hollywood Lettriste anti-art transplant starring Burt Lancaster plus nouvelle vague actor, Jeanne Moreau. Derailment in the purest sense of the word! However by 1960 Lettrist film techniques were, in a marginal way, present in Hollywood as after all, one of Hollywood's most celebrated directors, Orson Welles, in 1952, made a cinematic interview with Isodore Isou which will have done the rounds. Moreover, there was William Burrough's Isou-inspired film *The Towers Open Fire*; and the slogan *'Storm the Reality Studios'*, etc, which King Mob rather opportunistically deployed on a banner in a raucus London demonstration back in the good ole' days of 1968.

But we were situated in the 'right little, tight little island' of an England, determined on cretinism at all costs especially on the cultural front in regard to the rise and fall of form. A typical response was somewhat like: 'We are having nothing of that "Art is Dead" stuff. God Save the Queen"! Our previously mentioned early 1960s 'miniscule authentic band of late teen miscreants in Newcastle-Upon-Tyne' loved *The Train* correctly scenting 'an anti-art movie' - as we referred to it at the time - without *yet again* knowing about its Lettrist origins.

From 1950 onward all performance art was to depend upon publicity becoming the common denominator with the movie camera as ***the*** essential tool even in relation to the most acutely subversive acts which could end up with the perpetrators getting banged-up. Perhaps the first and finest, Michel Mourre and Serge Berna's anti clerical intervention during Notre Dame's Easter Sunday High Mass on 9th April 1950 was such a hit because that new invention, the TV camera was prominently filming the service. The convulsions which followed raged throughout the French press for at least 10 days, drawing in many of the big figures of the time, from stalwarts of the Communist CGT to the French Resistance to Andre Breton, etc. A pattern was thus set and 18 years later a slogan from 1968 exhorted: 'Make shame more shameful by giving it publicity'. In the following decades the world went publicity mad and alas subversion didn't escape its deadly embrace. It was if the individual stunt, even if exceptional, even if ending in jail, had become the be all and end all of insight; a brief flash of enlightenment and fame followed by nothingness. And there's the rub! Something more genuinely sustainable and collective must resolve this impasse, the brilliant act accompanied by lucid explanation which can resonate for a long time, sharpening many emerging minds already embarking on subversive thoughts and lifestyle; praxis thus begetting better praxis.

DAVID AND STUARTWISE

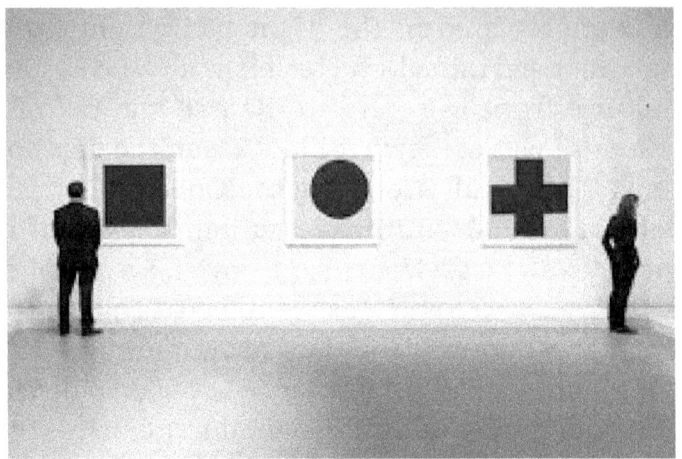

7 - THE PHYSICAL IMPOSSIBILITY OF DAMIAN HIRST IN THE MINDS OF THE LIVING

Stuart Wise
(2008)

'Shock Waves Rock Shares... but there's one man who just can't stop making money'

(Headline: *Evening Standard*, 16 Sept 2008)

The message from the sale was very timely and opportune, if only briefly so. Now that the public purse is all but empty why not 'butterflies' and 'spin paintings' as financial guarantors of last resort? Netting a fortune takes on an entirely new meaning as if E.O. Wilson's notion of 'natural capital' has finally come of age, with finance capitalism now become blood and flesh. So what next? An incredulous rescue package passed in the US Congress of a trillion wings torn off blue morpho butterflies? Or a universal shout, led by sacked banking employees, that installation/concept art is finance capital's new clothes, to be worn by the most susceptible to its bankrupt aura of creativity.

The mega success of Hirst's Sotheby sales, easily breaking all previous records for a 'living artist', unfolded against the backdrop of the most acute international financial crises the world has ever known, the ramifications of which are bound to be cataclysmic for everything and everybody, excepting art. This at least is the belief, or rather faith, that caused the usually philistine Channel 4 news presenter Jon Snow to let rip and say something interesting for a change. Interviewing a Sotheby's sales rep he asked what are we to make of all this, that butterflies are a safer bet than banks? The Sotheby's sale had bucked the trend of on-going financial catastrophe and for that reason must be regarded ideologically as the most important art sale there has ever been, even if it its salutary effect proved to be of short duration. For it briefly calmed nerves on the cusp of collapse and became the still centre of the storm, the one sound structure left in an otherwise tottering financial landscape.

The dream of a universal capitalism was embodied in the selling of sub prime mortgages to the desperately poor. But a dream which sought to anchor capitalism almost exclusively in that most basic need of all, a roof over ones head, had became the moment of sheerest hubris for latter day, free market capitalism. The shameless selling of the myth that there need be no ceiling to the aspirations of the poor under a system that was responsible for their poverty in the first place had, thanks to the success of the Sotheby's sale been decoupled, at least in the all important realm of appearances, from the only functioning market left, the art market. Universal home ownership, the idea of the home as limitless collateral, had amidst much blood and gore, surrendered the field, temporarily conquered by the 'democratisation' of concept art. With its last ditch promise of riches for everyman, it is finance capitalism's substitute for 'the poetry made by all'. From the German Dadaist 'Every man his own football' travelled through time to 'Everyman his own capitalist.'

Requiring no special skill, concept art had triumphed where Northern Rock, Bear Sterns, Lehman Bros, AIG, etc (and how many more etceteras are to come?) have failed and fictive values were reborn in the 'aesthetic' region that was once their prime home. But it is now just a creative nothingness, no matter how hard well heeled critics try to persuade us we are witnessing a veritable renaissance; a hype that is ridiculous and unhistorical though essential to the credence, and indeed, survival, of the 'value added' industries of Europe and America.

In fact weeks before the sales spectacular was staged, it had been cleverly advertised as a blow for freedom, an attempt to democratise the art market by subverting dealers, galleries, commission sales, and the cognoscenti it is necessary to network if one is ever to get to the top – or rather bottom, if one has by now any self-esteem left. Hirst, we are told, is sensitive to criticism and maybe he was out to refute a book that was written by an economist, Don Thompson, on the contemporary concept art market called 'The $12 million Stuffed Shark'. Here Thompson lays bare what one has to do if one is to succeed in the art business, a task requiring almost as much savoir-faire in knowing whom to flatter, and subservience to hierarchy, as in the court of Louis 14th, even though selling a product that historically has its origins in, if one goes that far back, to past revolutionary upheavals.

Whatever his private thoughts on the shallowness of court life, Watteau could never have cited revolutionary antecedents – and herein lies the paradox. Hirst likes to think of himself as an enfant terrible, an opinion continually reinforced by a press and a media as ignorant of real history as he is. Rather than break the mould, his destiny requires him to reshuffle the pack from time to time and so he now speaks of reinventing himself, perhaps blandly sensing a period is drawing to a close and that there is such a plethora of concepts as to devalue the market in a way that promise something else: a situation that has echoes of Marx's prediction there would come a point when capitalism could no longer valorize itself. It would be nice to speak of transcendence here but unfortunately one cannot, though it has to be said the valueless two-dollar bill struck to the head offices of Lehman Bros eloquently represents something stirring deep within which is far more likely to resonate in a meaningful way than anything Hirst has done.

The Channel 4 film crew members could easily have come up with the suggestion that a report on the bust Bradford & Bingley end with memorable footage of an upturned bowler hat on the pavement into which copper coins were being tossed. In fact the number of men and women queuing up to be photographed at the rear end of Wall Street's bronze bull is of far greater consequence than the record price paid for Hirst's 'Golden Calf', and which escaped the attention of media ironists. Nor did anyone seek to compare the clips of circling sharks on news bulletins, personifying the shorting of stock by hedge finds with the Tiger Shark sold by Hirst for an auction-busting price. Moral: a banker can be a shark but not an artist.

However, ever since the Saatchi brothers arrived on the scene, (Charles Saatchi commissioned Hirst's formaldehyde shark) art has been the interactive gloss energising capital's fictive gambling spree; the home becoming increasingly a time/space concept, rather than habitable, bricks and mortar interior. Women in fact became the chief victims of this home-centred revolution qualitatively different from the initial conservative bias of a free market version of kinder, kirche und kuchen originally proclaimed by Mrs Thatcher. Once the job of de-industrialisation was complete, the home, even more so than in America, became the motor of the economy, with women occupying a previously unimaginable, key role in its reproductive success - or horror. At the same moment women were becoming less biological, less mumsy, and of more 'direct' economic consequence to the economy. Housing was becoming more of a biological rather than economic fact, and, like the free market, part of the inviolable, natural order of things. The survival of the aesthetic fittest, central to a free market, makeover constructivism, granted a privileged position to women as aesthetic drivers of economic growth; rather more so than it did to men. Embraced with the all the fervour of the newbie, the involution of the aesthetic, rather than total revolution, became the reactionary answer – and one which the market eagerly seized on - to the profound alienation of women.

Go back ten years to when the Bradford and Bingley was still Britain's second biggest building society.. After demutualisation in 2000 when the building society became a bank with more freedom to borrow on the money markets, the bank called in the Saatchi advertising firm who promptly endeavoured to make its image less 'sexist', whilst in reality duping women more than ever. The image of staid British banking, represented by Mr Bradford and Mr Bingley, disappeared to be replaced by a young woman grinning knowingly at potential customers and whispering 'Aren't hopes and dreams fragile? But they could happen with the B 'n' B'. Offering mortgages to higher risk categories, the housing market became less family orientated and more about space and design and children; with the latter, as adjuncts to design, becoming 'clients' of their parents and free to butt out once the commercial deal of parenthood was foreclosed on.

All told, this development gave a money-orientated, psychological depth and persona to the housing market, different to the first wave of 'pragmatic' home ownership that began in the 1970s. 'Feeling at home' became more like being in a gallery, living within an installation or in a therapist's surgery. Promising a never ending high of rising prices, the housing market of the last decade played on opening the doors of perception. B and Bs final hubristic catchphrase, appearing in the windows of all its high street outlets, read 'Fixed, Done, Sorted'. Flanked by a life sized cut-out of a woman dressed in a smart green two-piece but still wearing a bowler hat, the time-honoured symbol of the B and Bs pedigree, it had a definite druggie ring to it.

More than anything else it is housing as an enduring, ever appreciating art/capital asset that has caused women to lose their social sense, rather more, it has to be said, than men for whom the home is less of an exhibit. Unreal housing aspirations then feed through into the reality of wrecked relationships once the more human part of the décor, the man, fails to live up to impossible designer expectations and is then blown out in the name of the unattainable. The dream home then increasingly turns into a lonely, solipsistic nightmare that no one dares enter. The present crisis is not just a seismic crisis for finance capital and its corollary, a bust housing market. It will also bring much needed, deflationary pressures to bear on the gullible expectations of new breed of power women, patsies for everything this aberrant, hopelessly lopsided, form of capitalism has to offer and that is now riven with multiple catastrophes.

One of the leading ideologists of contemporary feminism, Germaine Greer, was a late, very late comer to Hirst's cause. When we'd all had a bellyful of it, Greer was rhapsodising the inside of cows. This conversion on the road to Sotheby's, signalled Greer's awakening to concept art which she continues to make such a naïve hash of understanding 'the revolution of modern art'. The ever more cretinous Greer's worst performance to date has to be that following Robert Hughes' documentary, The Mona Lisa Curse, which singled out Hirst as the target for his opprobrium, she defended Hirst as the 'artist' who most epitomised Andy Warhol's dictum 'good business is the best art'. Greer condemned Hughes as a Stuckist for failing to realize Hirst's undeniable 'genius is in getting people to buy' his stuff – 'because the art form of the 21st century is marketing.' Aside from the fact Hughes is not a Stuckist, and rather belongs to a defunct tradition of the new (i.e. an avant-garde that has long lost any relevance as regards making 'us think and see more clearly'), what unites Greer and Hughes is infinitely stronger than what divides them. For both are wilfully ignorant of the truly subversive tendencies (e.g. latter-day Surrealism, Lettrism, the Situationists) unleashed by the rebellion of modern art, which sought the transcendence and realization of art through revolutionary upheaval and genuine mass creativity. And should either of them ever dig up this hidden history, both will be sure to hate it, as Hughes in particular opts immediately for the ultra capitalisation of art, preferring a billion Hirsts, an ocean of pickled sharks, and a universe of hedges any day to the prospect of an anti-capitalist revolution.

We were conscious of how Hirst, when he redesigned a boat he purchased in Chelsea boat yard, handed, in a self conscious way, much of the designing over to his wife, who wasformerly the partner of Jay Jopling, son of an ex Tory minister and owner of the White Cube gallery, (a free market tabula rasa of everything implied by Malevich's white cube). In the early days, in addition to letting Hirst get his leg over his girl friend, gave a leg up to Hirst, exhibiting his work in his gallery.

Never quite forgiven either by Saatchi or Jopling, for shorting the gallery circuit, Hirst eventually found a mentor in Frank Dunphy, an accountant from Dublin, who sorted out his tax worries and who had also managed the affairs of Peaches Page, the UK's first touring naked dancer and Julie Mendez and her Performing Python. Dunphy promised to make Hirst money rather than just save him money and Hirst eagerly took up the offer. Dunphy laid the ground for Hirst's dominance of the contemporary art market - though by now Hirst had already made the right moves and was now enough of a celebrity to get clean away with it. It was Dunphy who suggested Hirst go for a straight to auction sale at Sotheby's, bypassing the traditional route of an art gallery and hefty dealer's commission. Having successfully renegotiated Hirst's gallery contracts, ensuring the share of the proceeds from any sale increased from the standard of 50% to between 80% and 90%, Dunphy must have felt assured of further success in his campaign to further the rights of artists in preference to those of 'man'.

Hirst is hardly a populist in a political sense but it surely is significant that he prefers to do business with an accountant from a working class background to a Tory minister's son or an ex Courtauld graduate. It is the aristocracy of money he feels most comfortable with, not the traditional aristocracy of culture. And so on the night of the auction Hirst was to be found playing snooker with the former world champion Ronnie O' Sullivan. Had he still been a drinker he might have wound up with a more temperate Gazza. Hirst's choice of friends from outside the art market is symptomatic of the more democratic side of installation/concept art in so far as it requires no special skills other than the ability to make money. It is one of those enduring slogans that won't go away and inevitably entails the abolition of the role of artist. Now this is something Hirst utterly refuses to contemplate because he knows, as an arch commodity fetishist, that art is now interchangeable with money, and for him to accumulate yet more money it is absolutely essential that he never drops the pretence that art comes first, if he is to keep the Midas touch. It is not mere tongue in cheek sales pitch, for he genuinely believes his self serving deceit, and when push comes to shove he will stop at nothing to preserve the role of artist, every bit as much as his foe Hughes. Hirst is far more at ease with a tennis star like Navratilova, now turned installation artist, or John McEnroe, now a New York gallery owner, or Roman Abramovich, now the installation Tzar of the Russian art scene as well as boss of Chelsea FC, than with a 'proper' painter, or rather 'proper' dauber like Sidney Nolan, an artist much admired by Hughes.

Though far from the poetry made by all the sale was in principle open to all. This, at least, was the democratic façade, though in reality it was a highly select gathering and in that sense no different from the sniffy in-crowd Hirst wanted to short; thus in theory giving everyone the right to purchase his work. In fact the viewing screens in other rooms were only there for the show and only the favoured few were given access to telephones, a feature of art sales the TV viewing public have long been familiar with since art first started to be ramped spectacularly during the 80s, reaching its apogee when a painting of sunflowers by Van Gogh's was sold for a staggering £50 million to a private bidder (which later turned out to be a Japanese bank and marked the aesthetic nemesis of Japan's banking sector as property prices crashed and chronic deflation set in, despite massive public work projects of New Deal proportions that tested the limits of the absurd, like building inane airports in the sea in a country oversupplied with airport.

Then as now the salerooms broke into applause, when records were broken. I recall, at the time, someone on a building site saying he wished the principle could be extended to building operatives and that the more money we asked for, the more we would be applauded by our employers! There is a far darker side to this reactionary reinstating of core values than conventional concepts of artistic genius and veneration for 'fine arts'. Reverence for a hierarchy of talent and artistic order is even more spurious and falsifying than the 'everyman' concept art stuckists wish to overthrow: in the name of the one and only truth deified by history. Merely days after the conclusion of Hirst's Sotheby's sale, a convention of urban planners and architects gathered in Rome to honour the architecture of the Mussolini era and the robotic, Greco-Roman marble statutes ringing the Stadio dei Marmi. What we don't want is to be compelled, in the name of progress, to choose between stuckism and concept art, for both are pseudo alternatives leading to ultimate destruction in the long run.

That concept artists increasingly employ people has been of little note in Britain up to now. And we are not talking about a PA in a front office but an actual work force. Given the scale of the output of Hirst or Gormley it could not be otherwise. And yet we know nothing either of, or more importantly, hear nothing from, this workforce. Are these retainers too intimidated to speak out, fed up with low pay and being pushed about by half-assed geniuses? Or only too glad to be working for a master of the universe and even be willing to do so on an unpaid, voluntary basis? Does Gormley, by any chance, in his bleak house studios qualify for the title of the Gradgrind of concept art? And does Tracy Emin employ an amanuensis to write her weekly column in the Independent, merely throwing her (or him) the leftovers from her £120,000 a year salary she gets from the newspaper? Just to ask these questions poses a very real problem: why does none of this ever come out in this country? Is it because the notion of the individual genius, unsullied by trade, is just too strong a reflex here? Or are concept artists now celebrities and therefore just transcendent beings who breathe creativity and vacancy and have no need of anything more material?

Artistic idolatry in Europe particularly in France and Germany however also ineluctably gave rise to its opposite, an event that never happened here. Wagner is very much a case in point. Following the events of 1848, he turned his back on music and became a pamphleteer, before returning to the stage as the penultimate musician and rabble-rouser. He can be seen as the consummation of one strand of German philosophical idealism, the total work of art, as opposed to the total remaking of the world also posited by the same practical idealism. His influence was colossal, not least on the proto anti-poet Mallarme, who, in the last analysis, spun him into a remote territory as far from the overpowering drapes of the Beyreuth Opera House as its possible to be, the arena of everyday life. Thus Wagner was eventually returned to the insurrectionary streets of his youth, where everything was still to play for, and when he could still be found in the company of Bakunin, maybe even handing up the Raphael painting Bakunin mounted on a barricade during the Dresden insurrection – an act which would not have met with the youthful Wagner's disapproval.

There is nothing in this country remotely comparable to such a contradictory, almost incommensurate, development. It is so mind bending it easily risks being dismissed as utter nonsense in a 'common sense' country like Britain, which saw the rapid decline of 'revolutionary' romanticism following the deaths of Shelley and Byron. So excepting the late 1960s, art was never subject to critique here, and then it was rapidly overpowered and hushed up, like it never existed. Not however before the ideas had begun to seriously affect sections of the industrial working class, particularly in the north east, the ground having been prepared well by Jack Common, a figure comparable, in our time, to the 19th century German cobbler Joseph Dieztgen who floated his own version of the abolition of philosophy.

Concept artists are colossally ignorant, but if we grant that the beginnings of a critique of art here could be said to have arisen from within the ranks of the industrial working class itself, then it gives an added meaning to their anti-industrial bias and their effortless cooptation by finance. It is a fear of being exposed by the working class; not in the name of stuckism but by an imagination that intervenes and takes control of the social process. Although concept art originated in 1960s, in the early 1990s concept/installation art really took off and massively accelerated. It precisely coincides with the shocking decline in revolt and substitutes for that absence of revolt in a country growing daily more conservative because of the want of revolt. Consequently the ragbag of concept artists must fear the return of revolt because its imaginative implications could easily begin to outstrip anything they are capable of, and in fact already does so, despite going largely unrecognised. Already, individual, imaginative reactions to the financial crises is putting them in the shade - and not just because of their, now, transparent collusion with finance capital. To borrow a preferred Wall St. term, we could describe them as being hit by a 'double whammy'.

A few days prior to the Sotheby's sale, Hirst's face appeared on the cover of Time magazine (Sept 5/2008), prompted obviously by the coming 'sale of the century', or as Time magazine called it 'the biggest payday in the history of art'. The article was something of a revelation when compared with its average UK counterpoint, accustomed more to treating celebrities as mythical beings, the crowned heads of the entertainment life style we are all meant to worship and aspire to be. Detached from the humdrum world of commerce, money just naturally accrues to this uniquely English variation on media royalty. And when they are derided in popular 'Hello' type magazines, it tends to be over their waistlines and faulty boob jobs, not bank balances and shady business interests, which, as media angels, they are 'above'.

Time magazine showed up Hirst for what he was: an astute

businessman. Here we learnt for the first time he employs 180 people at six locations in England, including two massive facilities in Gloucestershire housed in converted Second World War aircraft hangars, with his scores of assistants executing his 'product lines' (sic) which are hugely profitable. Time also went on to ask 'where is the rule that the artist can't sell his work at auction', implying the problem really was one of productive capacity and 'that it was always likely Hirst would be the first artist to do that (having) the production capacity to supply a big sale'. This former Young British Artist (YBA) should now be in the Confederation of British Industry (CBI) and could be. However not because of the CBI's stuffiness in these matters, but rather on account of his links with finance and the City of London, which the CBI, as the champion of the industrial interest in this country, is still chary of, despite making concessions to it over the last quarter of a century.

Hirst is likely to be far less sentimental and it is possible he has a thing or two to teach the financial markets regarding the manipulation of the market for contemporary art. His diamond encrusted skull, 'For the Love of God' (reproduced on the front page of The Financial Times when it was first unveiled), was offered to the world's billionaires with a price tag of a $100 million. Hirst last year claimed that some numbskull had bought it for the asking price. However, it turned out the skull had been purchased by a still unidentified consortium of investors that included Dunphy, Jopling (owner of the Malevich invoking 'White Cube' gallery) and Hirst and that they will resell it after it has gone on tour.

Art critics today see more depths of inanity in what they are paid to look at, than at any other time in history. Indeed they are that depth, for without them the emperor would have no clothes. Restricted initially to a small coterie of nitwits, their influence over the past twenty years has broadened immeasurably and threatens to engulf the mass of a people that has lost its capacity for intelligent derision and subversive play. But for the critics' capacity to find meaning and purpose where there is none, the whole of installation/concept/performance art would go up in smoke. And so we are encouraged to see not the look of a financial shark in Hirst's cod-eyes, but that of a supreme ironist. And so a modern day financial Duchamp gazes out from a Leeds council estate. The prime lot at the auction was 'The Golden Calf' which set a new personal record of £10.3 million for Hirst. The hooves and horns are 18 carat gold and the head is crowned by a gold Egyptian solar disk. As the Time article said. 'this false idol is designed to flatter, beguile and parody the big swinging billionaires who are likely to bid for it. Not a bad bit of cheapo journalism and I began to briefly doubt myself. Maybe Hirst is taking the piss after all? However I then choked on his defence of his art, something Duchamp at his best would never have sank to, claiming his product was 'art first though, money second', adding 'I have taken the risk art will outshine the money.

Hirst's insistence on the 'democratic' character of the Sotheby's auction now takes on a whole new perspective even though it was far from democratic, despite whatever Hirst the shop keeper said to the contrary. He has gone on record as saying: 'I hate the way you walk into a gallery and say I want to buy a Damien Hirst, and they say "Who are you." I much prefer to be in a shop where you can just go in and buy'. In fact the sale was a strictly all ticket affair, though 21,000 visitors turned up to see what was most viewed pre-sale exhibition in London auction history. Sotheby's backed up Hirst's democratic posturing to the hilt. Oliver Baker, the senior specialist in contemporary art at Sotheby's, said the auction was an 'experiment that was breaking new ground' and that 'many of the works in the auction were small paintings that were affordable to many'. He concluded, 'From the outset Damien wanted to democratise this sale so everybody could be involved'. Cashing in one's chips at a last chance casino that is open all hours and to all, and wearing just a hint of a mocking smile as though it didn't matter all that much – is this the future the new global financial, market state, makeover is preparing for us? This at least was one scenario before it became apparent that the devastating anarchy of the financial markets was such as to rule out the possibility of even a state-regulated semblance of a return to old ways in the immediate future. If Hirst is as business savvy as he makes out, will he be able to make the transition to these changed times, perhaps aided and abetted by the likes of Greer who is more at ease with the notion of a social market economy than his present business manager Dunphy, despite his working class roots? Or will he simply become a casualty of the free market, this human capital write-down unable to reinvent himself in a way the times demand? And will a resurgent revolutionary movement be any better at critiquing him in a relevant manner? Questions, questions, questions and yet more questions, their number suggesting we really are approaching a cross roads. What has been said here is yesteryear. Or is it? Surely the broad outlines will merely morph while the essential of what's here will remain the same. Hirst will not.

8 - MECCANO ON CRACK (OR TATLIN ON CRACK)

A Psychotic Amalgam of Architecture/Sculpture/ Engineering

Stuart Wise
2010

Half in jest, it was suggested in *A Chorus for Corus* that an offensive Gormley colossus might eventually arise on the site of the former Redcar blast furnace to crow over the defeated steel workers of Teesside (who sad to say, have yet scarcely raised a finger of protest but, following union instructions, strove instead to prick the government's conscience); just as once a monument to the Duke of Wellington was erected on Stoodley Pike in West Yorkshire to celebrate the defeat of the Luddites and Nelson's Column sprang up in Trafalgar Square to ram home the defeat of the French Revolution. Whereas once obelisks and outsize statues of warmongers were the rule, today's displays of naked power increasingly shelter behind the mask of the neo avant-garde. And in fact the joke was on us, for we had spoken truer than we ever dared hope. Appropriately, on April Fools Day 2010, a joke was unveiled to the glory of the mayor of London, Boris Johnson, with the sculptor, Anish Kapoor, and steel magnate,

Lakshmi Mittal (who had just closed the Corus plant in Redcar), copping off with millions from the European Clean Energy Mechanism! Provisionally given a name, *The Orbit* it is to be the tallest 'sculpture' in the UK, standing a gigantic 115 metres and just short of the Eiffel Tower. Built 240 miles further south of Redcar on another industrially derelict site in London's east end, and now the Olympic Park, it will stand between the stadium and the aquatics centre. This was also payback time for Mittal; and the fact that it took just 40 seconds for him and Boris Johnson to seal the deal during a chance encounter at the Davos World Economic Forum suggests that Mittal had a colossus of a bad conscience to deal with (after all he is a big donor to the Labour party) and which was not good for his business reputation either. And so he jumped at the chance of supplying for free 19 million in steel bars weighing 1,400 tons that, for sure, will not be rolled in Redcar. It was a small price to pay for the thousands of wrecked lives on Teesside, for had the steel workers brushed aside set-piece, trade union opposition to the closure and taken the type of imaginative action that would have grabbed the world's attention, Mittal could have been forced to cough up an awful lot more to placate them and also persuade world opinion that he isn't such a bad guy. Thank goodness big art was there to salvage his honour this world class PR coup allowing him to win the first of the games gold medals! Whereas the lame responses of steel workers passed off virtually without notice when it so easily could have been otherwise, *The Orbit* instantly attracted worldwide attention that ideally should have been theirs and with a far more meaningful consequence to boot. Articles on the winning Arcelor/Mittal entry, saying much the same thing, appeared in the Chinese and Indian press, and even in a Burmese paper opposed to the military junta, a piece on the Orbit appearing below a photo of the president in waiting, Aung San Suu Kyi.

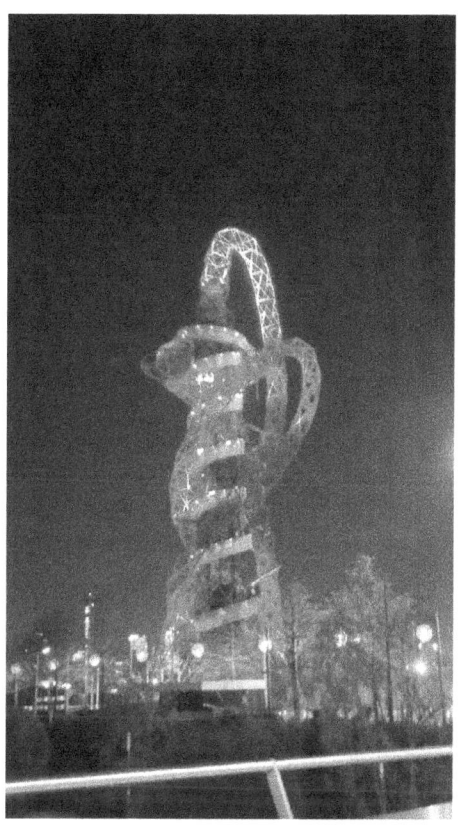

The official media response to *The Orbit* (and which could well become a brand logo for Arcelor/Mittal) was generally laudatory and that only goes to highlight the shameful depths criticism, never mind critique, has sunk to in the UK. Nor did any of the media big potatoes ever make the obvious connection between Mittal's *generosity* and the closure of the Redcar plant. The *Independent's* architectural correspondent Jay Merrick suggested there was something 'not quite knowable about the Arcelor/Mittal orbit's tower design'. Too right there was, which would have been obvious to anyone prepared to dig beneath the surface and confront capitalism and the realities of class struggle head on. Nor did anyone step outside the mental straight jacket imposed by the forthcoming Olympics to note that this candy floss gigantism was also aimed at kick starting the City of London's mega building projects, on hold and in the doldrums since the commencement of the economic crisis in 2007. True, the *Independent*, hinting there was just such a connection, directed its readers away from the front page article on *The Orbit* to look at a centre piece spread on the man 'who plans to tower over London'. The man in question is Irvine Sellars, a developer who hopes he will be able to complete Europe's tallest structure, *The Shard*, in time for the 2012 Olympics when 'the eyes of six billion will be on London'. But meanwhile there has been no movement whatsoever regarding the other metaphorical constructs like Land Securities *Walkie Talkie* and British Lands *Cheese Grater* and *Helter Skelter*.

In fact *The Shard* is something of an anomaly and is being backed, almost totally, by a consortium of Qatari investors who, even so, have transferred their investment, now a form of sovereign investment, to their government in Doha, a move that is indicative of the rise to power of state-owned sovereign funds throughout the world and an overall increased reliance on the state everywhere. Moreover *The Shard* is being plugged as 'living space' and 'the first artificial town' to Joe Public, because any mention of office developments occasions dread and stirs up fears of a resurgent financial trickery the poor will be left to foot the bill for when they haven't even begun to start paying for the present crisis. Sellars, accurately gauging something of the public's mood, reckons the other projected buildings are just 'office buildings' (i.e. casinos), though in fact well over a third of the building's floor space will be for offices. But whereas the other buildings are not something 'Londoners feel they can own', *The Shard* 'will be owned by Londoners' (a phrase borrowed from Ken Livingstone, the former Labour arty Mayor of London who was also drugged up to his eyeballs on a building high of high buildings. Of course neither meant nor mean their words to be taken literally and these words prompt a true act of appropriation. Rather, more's the pity, it is to be hoped Londoners will eventually get round to viewing *The Shard* in the same way as Lancastrians or Parisians, taking a great pride in what oppresses them, believing Blackpool Tower or the Eiffel Tower to be 'theirs'.

The same arguments are being used to justify the building of *The Orbit* and so the matter of how Londoners eventually will perceive this addition to the skyline becomes of greater importance than it ever would have been prior to the onset of the crisis. Above all, it must not be seen as a financial folly rate payers will be stiffed for in the years to come. At a stroke Mittal has relieved London rate payers of that burden. And so all is forgiven, especially by the Labour party and the redundant Redcar steel workers will just have to eat shit and like it. What's more, it must not remotely cross the public's mind that *The Orbit* is a pilot structure, kicking off a new phase of financial turpitude led by the property sector and deregulated investment banks, empowered like never before to do just as they fucking please because the public has had it well and truly drilled into them they are 'too big to fail'.

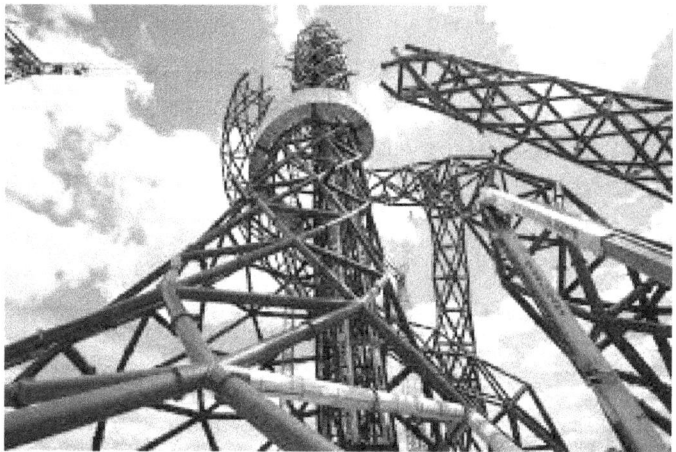

For the past twenty years, beginning with *The Angel of the North*, big art has been deployed to shift regional economies in the direction of financial services, property values, art and entertainment and away from making things and a passé industrial economy. And the bigger the art, the bigger the risks and financial con, with the next financial crises (which of course cannot be divorced from industrial capitalism) threatening to be of such a magnitude in fifteen years time, or thereabouts, that it will dwarf anything hitherto seen. *The Orbit,* variously described 'as beautiful as' a catastrophic collision between two cranes, or the Forth Railway Bridge dropped from a great height, or scaffolding stuck by a tornado, is a true portent of things to come. Pretending to be a cross-demographic fun tower, this really is not classic pyschogeography but psycho-architecture. Britain's answer to the Eiffel Tower becomes *Tatlin on Crack.* But whatever else, this mangled piece of latticed steel, violence and death psychedelia becomes, it must be constantly born in mind that it starts life as a truly appropriate symbol for the world's biggest drug fest, the Olympics. (It is to be hoped we are no longer swayed by the naïve drivel the games have anything much to do with fitness, healthy living - and games!)

There is no madness worse than what passes for common sense today; and this is where comparisons with the Eiffel tower break down. Eiffel's name inevitably cropped up in several reviews because his tower was the first clearly visible and successful engineering advertisement to date (from 1925-34 illuminated with signs from Citroen adorning three of the tower's four sides). Built as a decorative adjunct to the 1889 Paris exhibition, Eiffel's tower was not designed as a piece of public art, nor was it intended to remain in Paris more than twenty years, as part of the original contest rules stipulated that it could easily be dismantled. Eiffel's tower was cutting edge construction: in the late 1880s iron skeleton assembly was developed to unprecedented boldness and precision. Though appearing to be structurally unviable, its shapes initially modelled from wax, *The Orbit's* 'precise balance' is entirely down to computer programs developed by the engineering company Ove Arup's 'advanced geometry unit'. Though conjuring up ruin and impermanence that is the very last message *The*

Orbit's simulated molten steel is sending out. On the contrary *The Orbit* is here to stay, and if doubts are raised regarding its future, they only have to do with its post-Olympic role. In fact it gives the appearance of having over ridden the laws of nature, of being built in defiance of them – and chronic capitalist crises. Eiffel's tower was shaped by the forces of the wind, Eiffel having gained much of his knowledge regarding aerodynamic structures from his pioneering bridge over the Douro in Portugal. Kapoor's *The Orbit*, in contrast, appears more as the untrammelled product of the pure imagination that, unhampered by reality, has already taken power- 'imagination au pouvoir' as that rather imprecise slogan from May 1968 put it.

The toppling of global landmarks, especially the Eiffel Tower and the Statue of Liberty, whose armature was designed by Eiffel, has long been a feature of apocalyptic Hollywood movies functioning as safety valves, their number increasing in the past few years in response to 9 /11 and the deepening economic/ ecological crises. Like a deconstructed Twin Towers, *The Orbit* is an adjustment to apocalypse, the ground zero of an unchanging architecture of unfinished form in the process of becoming something else that will outlast even unimaginable catastrophe, just like the models of capitalism that have factored in crises. A master statement of zombie capitalism, *The Orbit*, under the guise of *daring innovation,* promises nothing but the same old shit. Once the Olympics are over, it is designated to become the centre piece of a new Olympic Park and a giant new Westfield shopping centre, a freak wave of their combined wand pulling in businesses, investors and house buyers. It's a forlorn hope because bubble capitalism – no matter how much it tries – cannot easily put its humpty dumpty back together again. An anonymous commentator from the North East - and not before time - adamantly claimed that the daddy of all big art, *The Angel of the North,* is locally ;still mostly despised' and that, if his experience is anything to go by, 'for years to come, every time the poor and downtrodden of the East End look up, they will see a big Fuck You.'

Tongue in cheek in *A Chorus for Corus*, we had even given Gormley's make believe statue on the site of the Redcar steel works, in perverse homage to Tatlin's *Monument to the 111rd International*, a name: "Monument to the Multinationals". Surprised, again our predictions hadn't been that far off the mark and Tatlin's name was bracketed in one *Guardian* newspaper article alongside that of the more frequently cited Eiffel. Of more concern was the fact that the benefactor wanted *The Orbit* to be called the 'Arcelor/Mittal Orbit': whereas Eiffel and Tatlin had naively lent their names to the cause of liberty, one believing in the USA, the other in the supposed anti-capitalism of the Russian Bolsheviks, Mittal is an unabashed defender of multinational capitalism at its most rapacious and greedy. But at least this renaming has the merit of exposing which side big art is on.

There is another aspect to the dysfunctional, de-sublimated engineering announced by *The Orbit* that relates directly to the counter revolution in the name of radicalism, launched against the most radical aspects of May 1968, and which has been alluded to above. Eiffel's achievements might be read as a criticism of the Ecole Polytechnique, France's *most prestigious* engineering institution to which he was denied admission. But what he did subsequently cannot be said to have its origin in a failed revolution, except very indirectly: his tower was erected on the Champs de Mars, site of a critical moment in the French Revolution when Danton and Desmoulins led a charge against constitutional monarchy. So, in a sense, the tower is, in so many words, stating publicly there is now no place for the *levee en masse*. Basically, however, the whole tenor of Eiffel's work is about transportation and getting from A to B in as short a space of time as possible. Like his railway bridge across the Douro gorge in Porto, it is utilitarian, and designed to lower the costs of the circulation of commodities. Not so *The Orbit*, which is a very different, and treacherous, ball game altogether.

The Orbit is the biggest and most twisted expression of the rage against the machine augurated by the reaction to May 1968 gone off in the wrong direction. It is the product of decades of counter-revolution posturing as its opposite. The initial blue print is really the book by Gilles Deleuze called *Anti-Oedipus* and not the provisional structures fed into Arup's computers: eschewing the need for e.g. wind tunnels, (ever the utilitarian, Eiffel was pleased to put his unnecessary tower to use as a wind tunnel in later life. Today, engineering and architecture increasingly tend in the direction of *'print'* engineering and architecture, with the software setting the machines that produce the parts awaiting human assembly. Permitting a far greater novel diversity than anything hitherto, this engineered parallel nature and computerized *diversity of life* is as close to a robotic process, from which every human feature, foible and delinquent moment has been erased as it's possible to get, short of automated replication.

Anti-Oedipus - Capitalism and Schizophrenia by two ace *wot-sits* of counter-revolution came out in 1974 in France. Its first chapter was entitled, significantly, *Desiring Machines* and in it all that had been challenged six years previously in May '68 is reinstated as subversive: from Tingely's auto-destructive machines (the original French edition contains a reproduction of one of them) to Caesar's compressed car bodies, to Arman's charred violins and so on. Becoming 'desiring machines' and therefore claiming to prefigure and embody post revolutionary values and society, according to this rubbish these 'art as resistance' machines push beyond the limits of capitalism, just as capitalism tends to do of its own accord, destroying traditional hierarchies in its ever expanding cycle of reproduction. A foretaste of things to come decades later, *Anti Oedipus* is on track to eventually substitute the studio for the factory, claiming 'desiring machines are the fundamental category of the economy of desire'. Echoing one of the most memorable slogans of May 1968, 'I take my desires for reality because I believe in the reality of my desires', the real aim of Deleuze and Guattari is the renewal of art, not its superseding in revolutionary praxis. Many years later John Jordan's 'Laboratory of the Insurrectionary Imagination' and 'irresistible machines' that would be used to such devastating effect (ha ha) in COP15 would jump out of this mummified bag of intellectual tricks. But in the last analysis so does *The Orbit*.

The ultimate chicanery and cleverness of postmodernism was founded on its initial ability to closely mimic the momentum of total social revolution; spreading bamboozlement in searching, well-meaning but still gullible minds whereby counter revolution would eventually triumph. Precisely because a perspective of genuine total social revolution was posited in the late 1960s, a seemingly grandiose totalizing of 'everything' was needed to counteract this drift if the grotesque system was to survive. An academically oriented postmodernism relatively quickly having done its worst could then submissively and triumphantly drift into an acceptance of a decadent epoch of financial wheeler-dealing based on debt; in short a bad totalizing amounting to utter bilge.

It was in France that this phenomenon *had to be* the most intensely practiced.....Ah but is it as easy as that? It wasn't as though the first dire murmurings of post modernism were seen by their instigators as 'reactionary', rather the opposite. What condemned them in an instant were mediocre contributions from equally mediocre individuals who had failed to live authentic lives, opting for cushy positions in a moribund hierarchy where no hard-headed choices had to be made. At best they were sympathetic voyeurs of the 'real movement'; afraid to say too much or, as Orwell put it in the context of Barcelona in 1936, 'always somewhere else when the trigger was pulled'. Academic qualifications mattered considerably to them as after all, how else would they have gotten published as they had nothing worthwhile to say?

Moreover, once the hard edge of a resolute critique of art had been vanquished, the stage was reopened to the illusion of artistic 'soft subversion' as a born again Fluxus perspective literally took over the world sweeping all before it. So much so that even a Raoul Vaneigem allowed himself to be invaded, giving interviews in 2009 to e-flux's Hans Ulrich Obrist who extols Beuys, Cedric Price, Gilbert & George etc, without Vaneigem raising a murmur and by way of reply even saying he offers 'a few texts to artistic friends'! Moreover, the guy is now sympathetic to some kind of low key collaboration with architects when once he (rightly) wanted to string the bastards up....

Attempting to cut through *Anti Oedipus's* pretentious crap after having chucked it one side in the early 1980s, we became aware how heavy industry and vast assembly lines no longer occupy the place they once did in Europe and America and whose presence is the backdrop to *Anti-Oedipus*. Following the publication of Marx's *Grundrisse* in the 1970s, many of us who studied Marx expected the immanent collapse of capitalism arising out of its inability to extract further surplus value from the industrial working class, with modern assembly lines being a transitional phenomena prevailing only so long as machinery was unable to perform operations of its own accord. However, this acted also as a timely reminder to industrial capitalists, who hastened to relocate production abroad where labour was far cheaper, and which offset the higher organic composition capital needed to continue functioning. As art increasingly replaced industry in *The West*, 'desiring machines', , rocketing in value, became more and more divorced from actual industry, their value, and that of the avant-garde in general, With Britain, in the process becoming the studio, rather than 'workshop of the world'. It was the credit / asset explosion that in addition made Britain the 'emporium of the world;, the unregulated credit mechanism, rather than the automation of factory production and *'reckless'* spending on basic utilities, including health, tended to breach capitalism's limits beyond which it was no longer viable, thus threatening to bring the entire house down. Especially in Britain, Ireland, Spain and America, housing became the driver of the economy. And along with this also went a pitifully failing, conservative counter-revolution of marriage and the nuclear family, plus a bull market in art / therapy, dotcom and creative industries. *Anti-Oedipus*, in retrospect, was just one of the primal fathers of this gory age that pretends to finality and the fulfilment of every desire. The book's formulations are so loose, obscurantist and pitted against the real spirit of 1968, that this verdict ought not to shock anyone with a smidgeon of historical sense.

A few comments to end with. As was fashionable at the time, the book ascribes a transcendent role to schizophrenia, viewing it as the chief psychological malady of the age but one that tends toward psychological overshoot, breakdown being also breakthrough - as had been outlined by the better part of Laing and Cooper in a more telling case story way in the UK in the 1960s. Becoming a catalyst for revolutionary change, schizophrenia is directly homologous to capital's tendency to suppress labour and become fully automated thus cutting its own throat, with 'capital's self-contradiction in motion' (Marx) eventually leaving it without a workforce to exploit, at which point it will collapse. But really the book's reactionary subtext amounts to little more than an attempt to claw back, in the wake of 1968, arts lost prestige, the expulsion of labour from machine production opening the way to the mass production of delightfully cuckoo 'revolutionary' artists on a scale never seen before. In so doing it is only pandering to a central myth of the crassest aspects of bohemianism, that of the mad genius sporting beard and beret whose shit one day will be worth millions and therefore worth investing in, as also such stereotypes serve the purpose of further marginalizing genuine subversive attempts at alternative lifestyles acquiring a more impressive, coherent and enlightened presence. Instead such lifestyles have been hunted down and are now on the verge of extinction.

But whatever became of schizophrenia? Already by the mid 1970s, depression was beginning to replace schizophrenia as the *maladie du jour,* with the incidence of depression since then vastly out weighing that of schizophrenia. Moreover there is every reason to suppose that depression is more directly connected with the continued existence of capitalism than ever schizophrenia was; this increasingly mass malaise is likely to become the psychological accompaniment to the dawn of post-human capitalism. At the same time schizophrenia has become mass, though it has not done so in the full blown 'clinical meaning' of the term and must be treated rather as a particularly extreme example of historical irony, when a thing desired becomes the opposite of what actually takes place and everything henceforth becomes split into two. However this typically dialectical contradiction is today stretched to the point of madness because of the defeat of contestation and becomes irreconcilable antinomy instead. Things exist henceforth on mutually exclusive planes: the surface in ignorance of the underneath, the bubble of consciousness oblivious to the sea of the unconscious on which it floats. The malignant product of a divided society and split personality, *The Orbit* is a Maldorean structure half way to being a world of cyborg engineering that threatens to walk abroad and play fearful tricks, this malformed 'desiring machine' turning, in a blink of an eye, into a nightmare of decay, rot and psychosis that owes more to Charlie Manson's mangling of a helter-skelter.

The unveiling of *The Orbit* provoked extreme reactions and gives an indication of the festering social antagonism lurking beneath the run-of-the-mill televisual. On the one hand we have the Mayor of London's bland economism and endorsement of domestic conservatism: 'we think we will be amply recouped after the games-time from the proceeds of renting out a very attractive dining facility at the top. It will be a corporate money-making venture (and) an internationally acclaimed family attraction'. And at the opposite extreme and from far lower down the social scale came the reply: 'this is Meccano on crack. Then, even better - and a wiser response - this then morphed into: *"Tatlin on Crack"*...

9 - ALL THE WAY TO THE BANK(SY)

SOME REFLECTIONS...
Stuart Wise
2015

Today we have little choice but to become socially inept on a massive scale and on every level of acceptable communication; thus putting an end to all subtle collaboration, especially the artistic/performance nexus. More than ever we need lines of clear demarcation like what Guy Debord tentatively hinted at in a letter to Yves Le Manach (23rd December 1972) on combating a more total, insidious 'decadent' recuperation, that fanfare of devious corporatism that is clearly evident in movements like neo-psychogeography:'But why must modern society recuperate anew so many revolutionary questions? Is it from gaiety of heart? It was certainly easier to recuperate us in the 1950s. As a result of recuperation, is not the ruling order becoming more and more sick?'
Years later and what has this sickness entailed?"
The outcome of Debord's sickness query has become a universe of fictive capital to the nth degree which has become inseparable from fictive creativity whereby permanent performance becomes the lynch pin of an increasingly inauthentic, hence unworkable and increasingly unbearable, everyday life. It as though the negative has been taken away from us, even extinguished or, so enmeshed with its affirmative opposite that it's become impossible to disentangle. Confusion really has created its own masterpiece; the masterpiece of an increasing

abyss. Hence Banksy.

With Banksy we have: An art that is anti-art seemingly beyond the realisation and negation of art / An anti-capitalist ultra-capitalism / The non-corporate corporate as his often telling street graphics morph into corporate praxis / a corporate subversion / Anarchy with a PR rep straight from Hollywood / An ultra-commodified anonymity / The clandestine guerrilla of subversive millionairing / Disappearance and invisibility as great career moves / Anonymous guerrilla action becoming a personality cult, an innovative publicity gimmick, etc, etc.,...... Enormous contradictions which are seemingly endless. Now without the promise sparked by an overpowering and recent profound subversive moment in the immediate past (as May '68 was in France along with the rest of the remarkable subversive moments elsewhere throughout the world around the same time) it is now necessary to invent the apparition of one along with the ghostly secondary reappearance of its own fictive aftermath. With 1968 the moment of true, radically clear-headed and profound anti-art was remarkably short-lived petering out by the turn of the 1970s. In no time a cynical compromise was obscenely set-up which helped keep the old world intact as seemingly daring innovation quite quickly acquired low key back-up from washed-up curators – almost fatally wounded by 1968 - and their well-off sponsors. Everything then changed in order to remain the same.... Unfortunately today we don't have any stunning, inspiring examples of authentic anti-art vandalism pointing to a new world. Instead, in its place, there's right wing, fascistic, (even anti-Semitic) bullshit scrawled on gigantic, banal, trophy neo-sculptures and the like, comments that aren't going anywhere, mere expressions of growing barbarism.

Banksy has a kind of Magritte-like talent and many of his pieces are very witty indeed causing startled passers-by to think more generally about how bad and lost things really are. For that simple fact alone he is way ahead of the vast majority of street neo-artists into mere banal decoration advertising little more than their own signature. There too the real conflict begins as Banksy sells vacuity back to the rich cynical shit-heads who administer (though hardly control) this dire state of affairs. No wonder he is hated by the rank 'n' file tags and pieces crew most of whom are honest though lost individuals who often never get out of trouble no matter how old they inevitably become, (see our account elsewhere on the *Revolt Against Plenty* web, 'Bradford's Eco-Peterloo. The Life and Death of Bill Posters'). Regarding the latter guy, it has to be said the early wall writings of Fisto are way beyond anything Banksy has been capable of, conjuring up some of the brief but real subversive spirit of the late 1960s, après the event. Without much further ado let's simply place here a few pointed facts about this super-hyped figurehead, this epitome of the hip neo-liberal persona whereby 'active creativity' is one of the most potent sales pitches...

Holly Cushing, Banksy's manager since 2007 used to work for Hollywood actor, Sean Penn. Financial records show she set up the limited company called Dismaland with Simon Durban who is thought to be Banksy's accountant. Sean Penn opposed the 2004-7 Iraq war and the war on terror. He was on friendship terms with Chavez and Raoul Castro. A typical pro sub-Bolshevik without a relevant critique of contemporary capitalism never mind an edgy critique of superstardom in general, Penn stood with Chavez when the latter supported President Assad against the uprising of 2011-12; an 'uprising' that is now so confused after the surreptitious intervention of the world's super powers, it's become just another horrendous calamity.

Banksy prints are released by Picturesonwalls, or POW, which is a London based (E1 not Bond St – where else?) gallery who represent Banksy. The gallery's logo is skull and crossbones, one of the crossed bones; decorators (not artists) paint brushes. Decorators' brushes indeed! HAH! Banksy could never have worked in the rough and tumble of building sites for years – never mind decades – on end. He would have found too much authentic truth and beauty there; one that is full of laughter and game playing; one that really subverts the grotesque artistic ego which is especially horrendous today in the epoch when art was declared dead decades ago.

Grey Fox is a PR company used by Banksy along with Pest Control which provides certificates of authentication. According to Jack Kresler of Christie's, London 'Pest Control is the sole governing authority; it's the mouthpiece of the artist'. It is said of Pest Control 'they seem to have an active policy of discouraging dealers buying and selling'. Forget about buying a work legitimately from the artiste - on the website of Pest Control there currently is 'something / nothing available'.

Today Christie's / Sotheby's Phillip de Pury sell only signed prints. Banksy is estimated by Forbes to be worth $20million. In New York's *Village Voice he sta*ted, 'success is a mark of failure for the graffiti artist': $20 million ...and the rest! Who are you Kidding! However, in fairness to Banksy there's still more of a human being in his soul than there is among the those truly fabulously rich, recent Internet moguls who have nothing but contempt for the Californian poor: one such CEO describing them as "grotesque...degenerate, trash." Internet Company CEO's rather younger than Banksy often in the mid 20s to the mid 30s at the oldest, who are into billionairing despising the paltry millionaring which Banksy represents. People like Travis Kalanick of Uber, Joe Gebbia & Brian Chesky of Air bnb, Mark Zuckerberg of Facebook, Amazon's Jeff Bezos, Keven Systrom of Instagram along with uber-pirates like 'rebel' Kim.dotcom...and the list goes on and on!!!!!

Banksy has a seemingly casual attitude to copyright encouraging the reproduction of his work for your own personal amusement, so it's with "regret" that he finds himself having to say whether pieces are real or false. A framed print appeared on Banksy's website the day after his 2007 exhibition at Sotheby's when his work soared well above the auctioneer's estimates. The caption on the print, which shows auction goers bidding up prices, reads, 'I can't believe you morons actually buy this shit'. In the immortal words of that wonderful sarcastic tart, Mandy Rice Davies, 'Well, he would say that, wouldn't he'. Banksy is very aware of the great creative hole at the heart of everything today and working in and through an ever increasingly desperate nihilism, sells the emptiness back to the '1%' in real style. Even intuitively aware of the 'theological capers of the commodity' (Marx) Banksy becomes a fascinating, phantom God of Emptiness fronted by the sheer worship of money).

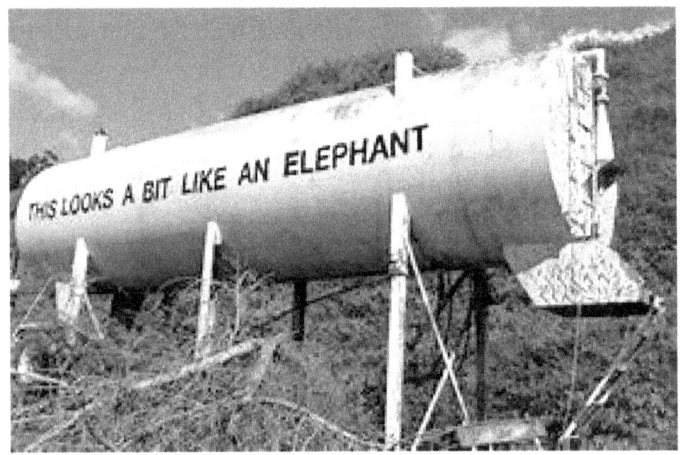

Banksy set up a pop-up stall in New York's Central Park selling 100% authentic original signed Banksy canvasses for $60 apiece. 2 buyers bought three works whose real value was estimated to be $200,000. The pop up stall was meant to be a comment on capitalism, authenticity and the art market. Banksy signs a water tank overlooking the Pacific, the caption reading 'THIS LOOKS A BIT LIKE AN ELEPHANT'. tank became an instant tourist attraction, a media design firm instantly buying it from the city of Los Angeles with plans to remove it and sell it. A homeless person was living in it and when Banksy found out, he gave the homeless man money to buy an apartment and refused to authenticate the work. It crashed in value ending up in a scrap yard. All very clever, smart stuff making out he's anti-money and generous to the poor when basically Banksy is a ruthless, inauthentic manipulator. In reality Banksy had to look at his projected image first and foremost and in order to keep his 'subversive' prestige intact he couldn't do anything but buy a gaff for this homeless guy. Evidently when he wants rid of somebody - i.e. if they criticise him - Banksy pays them off handsomely. When people get rid of us occasionally for ordinary, though usually accomplished building work, etc., they invariably rip us off refusing to pay up a damned penny. So which is the more real experience?

Regarding copyright, there is now on-going hostility between Banksy and the French neo-artiste, Blek Le Rat who way back was influenced by the ubiquitous screen prints from the uprising of May 1968 particularly the well known simplified stencils of CRS riot police. Banksy has a similar obsession with police as most graffiti neo-artists understandably do. His Kissing Coppers daubed on the walls of a Brighton pub sold for $575,000 in 2014.This really is a maimed expression of the poetry made by all falling back into the old copyright scene beloved of a culture scene on steroids. Down at the bottom where we are located we freely take from each other in and out of collective effort and individually unequivocally glad to see an idea you once had bearing fruit elsewhere. This is not a rip-off as money making doesn't come into it. What galls us is seeing time and again our ideas constantly ripped-off, used and abused in the media – mainly via journalistic scum – who don't ever have the decency to mention the source, though would do so if the source was part of the official hierarchy culled from some frikin' fink who invariably props up the system in one way or another. Banksy, of course knows who we are and therefore his real Elephant in the Room minus the William Morris wallpaper.

Banksy filed for trade mark protection with UK's Intellectual Property Office. It looks as though Banksy did this to stop his brand being used to market cleaning products: i.e. 'Banksy cleaning fluids, get rid of stains and graffiti the easy way', etc, etc. Recently a good internet reply on Banksy read: 'He's a guy who says that until the inevitable collapse of capitalism we should all go shopping. He'll be advertising County Life butter next alongside Johnny Rotten'. However that would reveal his identity. Or maybe not; in fact an even more obscure though tantalizing anonymity could be the cleverest of sales pitches. Doubtless Banksy wouldn't be as dumb as to feel sorry for the Royal Family as a rotting Rotten now does. But you never know as Banksy is now shaking in absentia hands with absolute finks like Damien Hurst who acted out his part in Dismaland. Even The Financial Times rather smartly said of Banksy, 'The stencils provide the marketing; the gallery walls the cash flow, a virtuous cycle of profit and publicity'. Too right - this really is how he keeps his 'virtue' and street cred.

In June 2015 Banksy's Silent Majority spayed onto the side of a mobile home during the 1998 Glastonbury festival sold for £ 445,000. The rest of the caption reads, "It's better not to rely too much on silent majorities - for silence is a fragile thing - one loud noise and it's gone" Like so much of Banksy's 'serious' statements wat-da-fuk does this mean? Empty nonsense. Banksy's trajectory has been to gradually mould genuine subversion into a hip form of avant-garde neo-liberalism, part of that "terrifying subtle" syndrome previously mentioned in regard to the dismal reality of corporate totalitarianism. His comments sound so deep and yet are no more than a return and reinstatement of gallery product, a having your cake and eating it post modernist vacuity so typical of the hip neo-liberal individual. In late August 2015, Banksy said of Dismaland, "It doesn't so much ask the question, 'What is the point of art now?' as ask, 'What is the point in asking, "What is the point in art now?" Again: wat-da fuk does this mean?) If Banksy really wanted to create a stink even at this late stage in his meteoric career – one that would rock-on down through the years – he could turn on his big money aesthetes by simply getting a gang together to trash one of their rich condominiums – and issuing a lucid statement alongside an example of coherent vandalism and anti-art subversion…..But he won't do that, will he???

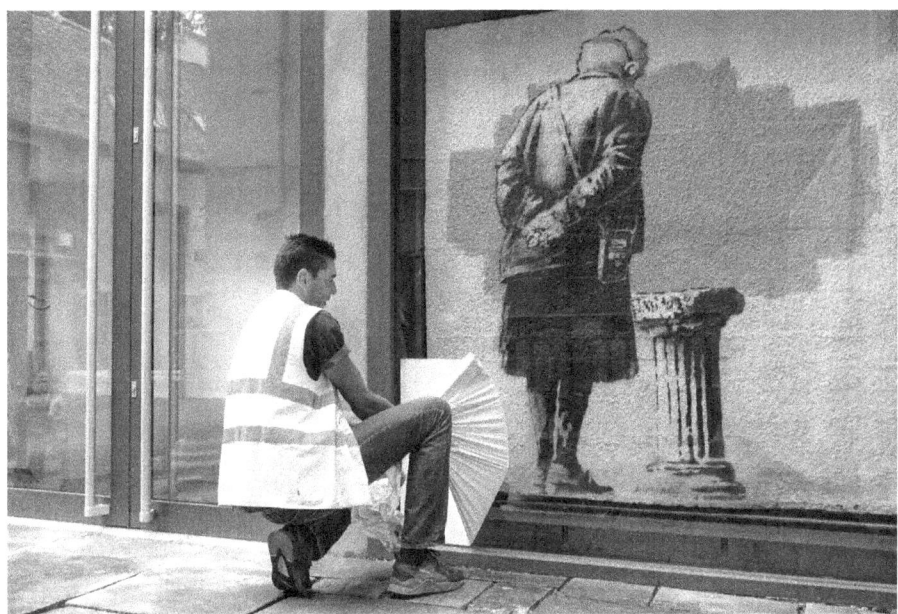

Banksy's Folkestone piece was vandalised in August 2015. Entitled 'Art Buff', it showed a middle-age woman wearing headphones, hands clasped behind her back, gazing in worshipful awe at an empty plinth. It was hardly knowing vandalism, the attacker painting an erect penis on the plinth, Folkestone Council anti-graffiti squad rapidly moving in to clean the 'obscene' addition off the hallowed spot in the grounds of a local park. Art Buff's estimated value is reckoned to be £300.000 and had created a surge in tourist numbers visiting Folkestone's Triennial Festival. It can be reckoned a try out for what would happen on a much bigger scale in Weston-Super-Mare. Tracy Emin is attempting to pull off a similar stunt in Margate. What the guy who vandalised Art Buff should have done is put a crude cut-out figure on the plinth with Banksy stencilled over the figure. Now that would be a really cutting edge and a real contribution which could help revive the essential revolutionary critique of art. As for Tracy Emin: Well, she won't get anywhere as like all the rest of the dumb fuk, contemptible YBA's of the mid to late 1990s they simply didn't have a clue as regards a developing subversive critique of the totality. Most were Blairite

New Labour in persuasion, though Emin quickly returned to the Kentish Tory fold. Present day hip neo liberalism, on the nervous edge of disintegration needs attributes and responses far more advanced. A figure like Banksy is just the ticket able in his Dismaland A3 brochure to include strains of South West England anarchism (which is indeed better than most contemporary anarchism's) plus ASLEF oriented rail workers' strikes that significantly don't involve an essential critique of unions which was so prevalent in France Goes Off The Rails.

Basically, Banksy represents the ultra recuperation of people like us, indeed even to the very core of our beings who of necessity engage in a praxis which encompasses an often hour-by-hour clandestinity, endlessly engaging in disappearing 'tricks' simply to keep the heat off our backs of an everyday life where almost by rote, you are ever looking over shoulders for the filth, security guards and the like, ever repeating to yourself Brecht's dictum, 'No, no, never, never answer the door'. As for ourselves we carry on belonging to something like William Blake's and Samuel Palmer's Society of the Ancients. Ah, and then the BIG difference: Banksy turns creative moments into art and cultural specialism's acceptable to a virulently moribund status quo, utilising essential disappearance tactics as a PR stunt, who in a flash becomes a commodified Houdini or more potently, a commodified Jack Shepherd who vanishes from the arms of the military on the way to Tyburn Tree... and all to the wonderment of a captive, passive audience.....

The changing tenor of the times worked behind our backs. Not only couldn't we exist through any professional career or role, ineluctably along with others, we more and more distanced ourselves from all counter, oppositional milieus, anarchist, ultra-leftist, situationist, etc., if only because we were unable to fit in with the increasingly rarefied, hot-house temperatures such groups thrive on, remote from that essential: a turbulent but real everyday life in and among all those who increasingly just to say exist, clinging-on at the sharp end as we endlessly keep disappearing into the disintegrating masses. And, needless

to say, light years away also from academic theorists no matter how interesting some of their ideas might be who immediately tend to shame us by pulling rank castigating inadequate use of the English language, etc. Moreover, the type of creeps WHO NEVER GET THEIR HANDS DIRTY, most needing a good haymaker to the jaw to bring them back within the realm of acceptable behaviour. Permanent night and day occupancy of that by now very unfashionable coal face - as it were – always but always makes all the difference in the world.....)
And so to Dismaland

That buffoon of an art critic Jonathan Jones (Now that's a guy who really does hates us) today looks askance at employee strikes in 'venerable' institutions like the National Gallery (and incidentally no different to another buffoon name of Anthony Gormley who also doesn't support such strikes) said in The Guardian, 22nd of August 2015 - obviously needing to brush-up his tarnished image - opportunistically goes a bit situationist in 'all that is false about Banksy' launching an attack on Dismaland in Weston- super-Mare, saying: 'It claims to be 'making you think' and above all to be defying the consumer society, the leisure society, the commodification of the spectacle, Disneyland packages dreams, Dismaland is a blast of reality.' This is ironical seeing Banksy's ideas were sufficiently grounded in King Mob (without Banksy ever having the decency to mention such an excrescence) having purposefully lived for many a year during the 1970s next to the huge Same Thing Day after Day, etc., graffiti on the Hammersmith & City tube line as well as more recently probably having taken note of the original English SI, Charlie Radcliffe inspired, Disneyland piss-take poster seeing it was finally posted on the RAP web only a year or so ago having been lost in a Newcastle –upon-Tyne attic for many a decade.... For sure we do realise that Banksy has been playing with the theme of Disneyland for many a year having, among other things, clandestinely placed a life-sized replica of a Guantanamo detainee in Florida's Disneyland which took 90 minutes for security to remove. But did Banksy know of another transcendental collective precedent and one that wasn't about bigging up a star in the making? Again in some pamphlet of ours (quite forget which) we recounted the great invasion of the Florida site by a bunch of yippies around 1970 who imaginatively vandalised and re-arranged many an exhibit including the exquisite re-shooting of a then cranked-up, mechanised Abe Lincoln. Attacked and beaten up by security guards most of the insurgents did however manage to make an anonymous escape, so we'll never know anything more about such a creative high as, for sure, it was brilliant. And seeing we mention Newcastle, on the one hand, isn't Dismaland merely a surreal variant of sculptural post modernist attempted city regeneration not that different to Gormley's stuffy and obnoxious Angel of the North meaning oodles of money will pour into the decaying seaside town of Weston-Super-Mare for a short period of time? And then: Nothing!

On the other hand, isn't Dismaland little more than the extension of a Fluxus art event or Happening in say the mid-1960s waning in comparison with the direct, clued-in, provocative intervention that can start a prairie fire; detonating a chain reaction throughout an awakening population that means real active rebellion is simmering even if not yet coming to the boil? Isn't Dismaland just an alternative passive tourist attraction that doesn't set the processes of real liberation in motion? All Dismaland is doing is bigging-up the flagging careers and sales expectations of somewhat outré neo-artistic specialists; a further boost if you like to repeat after repeat of neo-punk phenomena. Moreover most of these neo-artists assembled here don't even make their own rubbish as that onerous task is farmed out to skilled crafts people no doubt sufficiently deferential to the neo-liberal, neo-cultural reality. As for other 'cultural' fields, not for nothing has Banksy selected the anti-Putin, Pussy Riot that came out of the worldwide protests of 2011. Of course these gals were / are brave and their account of the 'new' Gulag is fascinating and harrowing but typically they have been taken up by western celeb' culture which, like all cutting edge critique from Russia since the late 1960s the protagonists somehow cannot see through. As for home-grown territory, well, of course, it had to be Sleaford Mods, who in the performance shop window are so anti PC that, 'fuck' 'shit' 'cunt" spills over in every other lyric? And while we are into the obligatory swearing, it would seem similar fucking cunts going by the name of Rawfolds (named after the desperately heroic Luddite attack on Rawfolds Mill near Bradford around 1817) perhaps weren't invited and West Hartlepool's Kill the Poets, it seems have gone soft on the stage. (Is it necessary here to mention Apollinaire's initial, anti-cultural Assassinate the Poets epigrammatic call to arms in what was once an anti-art North East?)

The banal realisation of so much of what was once the uncorrupted negative at the heart of capitalism, things like power to the people, education for all, free medical care, etc., and which later was to include Lautreamont's great dictum: "the poetry made by all and not by one" were sullied from the get-go through certain lamentable lapses and badly thought through arguments. In Lautreamont's case it was the deployment of that damned word POETRY which superficially can mean everybody becomes an artist as understood in all its present day banality minus the essential transcendence of art. Perhaps it can be said great subversives were also scared of themselves policing their deepest insights through lack of clear explanations, lapses that late capitalism could ruthlessly accommodate decades later, lacking as these 'seers' often did, a razor sharp cutting edge that could counter all future dissimulation. (To take one example, hadn't Andre Breton decades ago condemned Isodore Ducasse for hiding behind the 'execrable' aristocratic name of the Comte de Lautreamont even though it was probably Ducasse's play on the image of the amazing Lord Byron?) Equally it could be said, how on earth could Rimbaud delete these following lines from his final version of A Season in Hell? 'Now I can't stand mystical beliefs and stylistic strangeness. Now I can say art is folly. Our great poets just as easily: art is folly. Hail beauty.'

In between there's the missing link: In 1986 - the time of France Goes Off The Rails - the Internet in any real mass sense did not exist so little could we realise that nearly three decades later billions of individuals would create their own artistic / performance-oriented persona despite meaning sweet fuk all, least of all as expression of genuinely individual-cum-mass creative, active impulses.

Firstly however, we must acknowledge and honour those truly courageous, creative geeks; those socially engaged hackers etc., many of whom have ended up in jail having remained true to the original utopian promise inherent in the early years of the Internet. There's also many a stirring blog out there and surely we are all grateful for that. Moreover, it could be said we're hypocritical here as we've also created webs to get our unacceptable ideas across, though we've had little choice in the matter, seeing that the once reasonably common alternative bookshop that stocked our pamphlets has, with hyper-gentrification of bricks and mortar, disappeared eons ago. Many too are the individuals who've promised to publish our tracts in dead tree format, most also disappearing in a puff of smoke (and mirrors) usually after a bout of hi-jacking.

The evolution of the Internet has been clever and ominous at one and the same time. Given a quick start on the back of great utopian hopes of liberation, like freedom from money and the constraints of political economy in general, a fledgling internet never amounted to anything like a critique of political economy in the sense Marx or Bakunin would have grasped it. It did though embrace a subversive, freewheeling life style emanating from American late 1960s counter culture. Fifty years later and that counter culture in California's Silicon Valley has been turned inside out pointing not towards the abolition of wage labour, money, value, the state and commodity production but to its exact opposite: an ever expanding plutocratic nightmare even worse than the robber-baron phase of mid to late 19th century America as we head towards a new feudalism of digital billionairing and analogue beggars. A place where the Internet magically floats outside of time, space and history – an unplace – far removed from a suffering but vibrant, somewhat egalitarian everyday life which still just to say, exists among those at the sharp end. Their ideal is an aesthetic psychogeography of trophy architecture on fabulously false, off-shore islands, floating 'utopias' with a nod towards Charles Fourier, never forgetting that Los Angeles was founded in the mid 19th century on the shell of a Fourierist commune. Nowadays and Straight Outta Compton these are Xanadu's of cyberspace cast adrift on silent seas forlorn, only to be then filled-up with money-mad geeks cut-off from churlish street shit.

Yes, these Internet innovators were finally able to market revolt; nay make it their lynchpin; the un-club, the anti-establishment establishment, disruption as the motor of billionairing where Cool has also morphed into its opposite becoming the orthodoxy of networking........ Inevitably the aforementioned un-places had to be horrifically re-invented meaning late 1960s counter cultural festivals like Burning Man in the Nevada's Black Rock Desert have become low profile but hyper-capitalised events served-up by celebrity chefs with everybody of 'importance' billeted in air-conditioned yurts. Elsewhere in San Francisco, Twitter's new downtown plush but casual looking office has a dining area sickenely named The Commons replete with gourmet cuisine. Truly what the old French Situationists acutely divined, 'We are on the same path as our enemies' is even truer, heading towards a destination – pace a slogan of the May '68 uprising - where 'Everything is Permitted' or, rather, it's cool to smash up everything, and rip off everybody but where money, status and the new informal, casual uber-elites of 'disintermediation' – whatever that means - are worshipped. As for *France Goes Off The Rails*, perhaps the most incisive graffiti of December 1986 - in retrospect pointing so brilliantly and ominously to a darkening future - is simply 'ISOLATED......KILLED OFF' and the real anthem for future doomed youth vis-à-vis having no future. An unravelling where instead of autonomy, the automaton is taking over via the loneliness of an ultra-commodification so intense that societal autism is plumbing new depths of depersonalisation disorder characterised by privatised narcissism masquerading as isolated 'perfection', making, in comparison, The Lonely Crowd of 1950s radical American sociology appear as warmish conviviality. Thus we remain "alone together" via an Internet where 'the more we connect and communicate the lonelier we become'. (Keen)

And yet such praxis is cleverly disguised by a re-wiring of business behaviour appearing to give everything away for free via an innovative "personal revolution", reimagining oneself as aesthetic substance when it's all about filthy lucre, where the personal is the economic, where narcissism and generalised autism merge; a selfie-centered delusion. In an age lousy with celebrities, everybody can be deluded into thinking they are an artistic genius just at the moment of utter artistic bankruptcy. All is promo; a gift economy where profits are only for awe-inspiring Internet plutocrats; where the poetry made by all masks and becomes the grim fact that contrary to appearances, everyone is clouded in obscurity as every laughable 'creative' is shaken down and devastated. It means that a vast proletarianisation and dispossession is underway endlessly trashing the millions of re-imagined artists, writers, photographers, sculptors, dancers, singers, musicians and what have you all lined-up to be symbolically offed, offed and offed again......... One day hopefully all these schmucks will awaken to the giant con they've been subjected to and unfortunately believed in. And then maybe – just maybe – we can have a real ball the like of which no contemporary reimagining could possibly match. Roll on Utopia. Hail beauty...

KING MOB: THE NEGATION AND TRANSCENDENCE OF ART

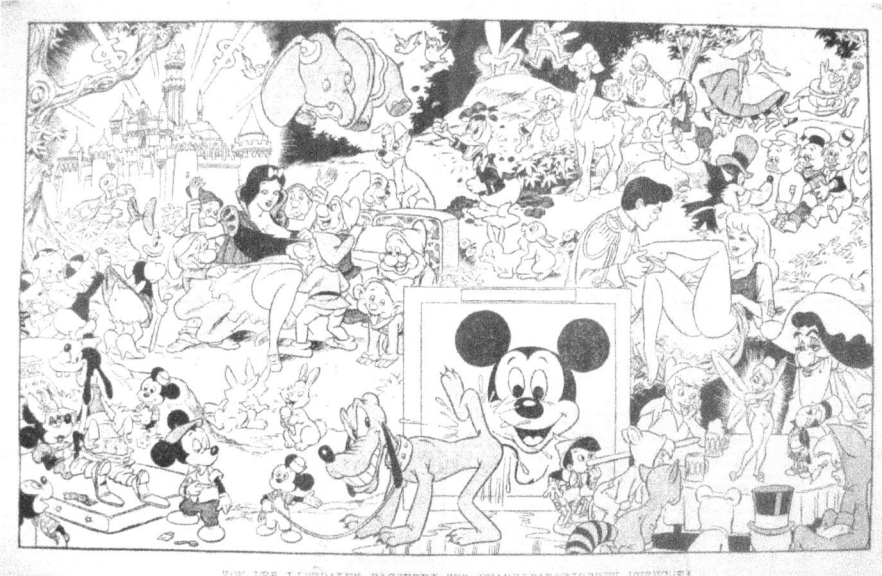

Above is a poster put out by Charlie Radcliffe of the English section of the Situationist International around 1966-7. Also true for King Mob a little later it can be said we always collectively deployed filth and the worst of lavatory humour in provoking pertinent anti-capitalist points of view, hence the dollar signs beamed from the fairy castle in the background. Moreover, and essentially there was no emphasis on any form of monetization. Indeed at the height of Situationist subversion we always emphasised that everything should be free. In comparison Cinderella's upturned coach is much more acceptable in Banksy's Crash (below) at Dismaland in Weston-Super-Mare where lithographs of the 'art object' were sold for between $400 to $500 to customers - and not viewers.

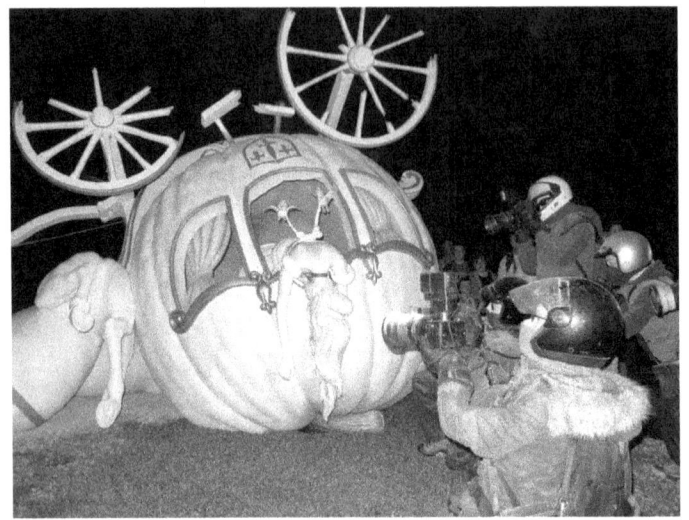

10 - MAYAKOVSKY AND TATLIN

A Catastrophic Social / Creative Impasse

(....by way of the personal tragedy of Mayakovsky)
Dave Wise
1973

Of all the Futurists and Constructivists, Vladimir Mayakovsky was the only avant-gardista to have been in the Bolshevikh party and to subscribe to the theory of the social revolution well before the Russian revolution of 1917 had occurred. He was no fellow traveller. As early as 1905 Mayakovsky was jailed for being a member of the Bolshevikh party only to leave the party soon after his release as he felt the Bolshevikhs didn't understand what he was getting at artistically. From then on, he remained unto himself, alone (as it were) and Mayakovsky's vision of the coming revolution (a very personal one) is seen in *A Cloud in Trousers*. He was thus the first of the avant-garde to have reservations about the Bolshevikhs; reservations which in the heady years after 1917 became more and more pronounced: from the satire of *Re-Conferences* to the bitterness of *The Bedbug*. Wanting freedom – personal freedom – at all costs, his critique revolved more and more around the bureaucratic rigidity of the party. The unresolved contradiction between his sense of duty to the Leninist vanguard and the need to fulfil himself ended in suicide. The conflict was agonising.

I have no intention here of deifying Mayakovsky, nor do I suggest that Mayakovsky's particular historical contradiction / intervention in the revolution has any relevance today in the exact form or path it took. Thus such 'poets' like Adrian Mitchell, Adrian Henri and even Roger McGough, who in some ways, consciously or subconsciously, have modelled themselves on Mayakovsky's example, have long ago had their day. Mayakovsky's originality lay in a moment of time pregnant with the disintegration of all artistic form; that moment when 'creativity' was beginning to slip the leash from 'the ball and chain of art', as Andre Breton eloquently put it sometime later. Since the conclusion of the Second World War we have been witness everywhere to a repetition of cultural disintegration – now largely press-ganged, and institutionalised in the service of consumer production which hasn't had – or could have had – any of the original vitality of Mayakovsky's day, though perhaps its momentum is more important historically for the coming total revolution chiefly because this repetition is everywhere.

Mayakovsky's tragedy though remains relevant as it is the tragedy of a man or woman caught in the horrible nexus of a society without hope, one that gives no satisfaction on any level; in work, in personal love life, even in what passes alas for pleasure and creativity. Is it a bourgeois tragedy? About 150 years prior to Mayakovsky's suicide, Goethe wrote about another suicide in *The Sorrows of Young Werther*, which Lukacs in *Goethe and his Age* says expresses a predicament which will remain until bourgeois society is overthrown. In some ways Mayakovsky's tragedy echoes young Werther's, though Werther as a young Jacobin was situated in the still feudal society of Germany in the late 18th century. However, Werther's subjective extremism appealed to individuals in the two major bourgeois democracies of the time: France and Britain.

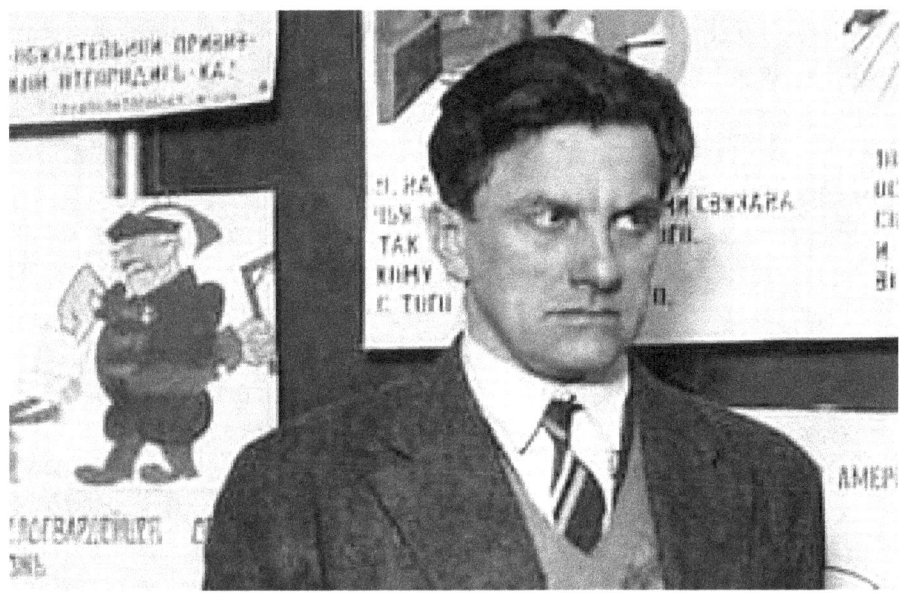

And in response to the above, common enough ripostes will loudly but sadly take the form of 'Surely the two suicides cannot be compared because Mayakovsky's took place in the context of a socialist/communist society?' And there's the rub. His suicide must testify to the truth of the reality that the so-called revolutionary communist society wasn't revolutionary or communist in any meaningful sense, which is why we cannot deploy the term 'communist' any longer for what we want because such description has become contaminated, lacking veracity. What Mayakovsky was confronting was in reality an emerging, increasingly hideous bureaucratic state-capitalism he found too painful to live with.

In a post social revolutionary society I don't think there will be suicide in the sense we recognise today. No doubt there will be individuals who may want to end their lives, but not because of a desperate, imposed painful alienation they have no control over. Today, those 'revolutionary' individuals around us, battered by the reflux we are now painfully experiencing post the end of the glorious late 1960s, insist on the right to commit suicide but do no more than repeat in an inevitably vulgarised manner the debates of the Enlightenment, in particular David Hume.

Opposed to the taboos of the church, radical liberalism on such points then had real meaning. Today in conditions of intensified exploitation it means life hasn't any meaning and 'Is there life before death?' as the King Mob graffiti put it becomes more poignant than ever.

Moreover, in conditions of increasing inhumanity how far is the 'right to commit suicide' from 'the right to starve?' In Herbert Marshall's book on Mayakovsky, Maurice Bowrie says, 'In the end the struggle was too much for him, and in a moment of deep melancholy, such as was not unknown to him, he shot himself. Many guesses have been made why he did so, but as with most suicides it was probably in the last resort inexplicable'. All such comment fits in well with Mayakovsky's epitaph in *Pravda* which said his suicide was due to personal reasons! The fact is Mayakovsky's death was like Van Gogh's, an individual 'suicided by society' in Artaud's telling phrase.

And yet Mayakovsky's last poem – if one can call it that - had the upbeat, chirpy title, *The Coming Bright Decades*. So what were the particular circumstances which forced the guy into a kind of fixed form of Russian roulette? Mayakovsky's will power cannot be doubted. In fact there was an over-will. His egoism or hedonism, such a common feature of the artistic avant-garde (and ,by the way, a constant in other avant-gardes too, not least the political) was loudly proclaimed, 'I – Mayakovsky – versus the Universe'.....And it was an I, I, I, I, all the way but an 'I', an ego, on a journey that became more and more frustrated as the path (the quest) became more and more blocked and as he reacted to the all the different environments around him: those who blindly worshipped machines; agit prop; bureaucrats; and finally to his own unbearable loneliness, standing there, perhaps ahead of most people in the world. 'I am so lonely as the single eye of the one-eyed walking towards the blind' (notice he is only one-eyed), or in *The City* a 'poem' screamed out in 1925. 'I'm fed up – I'd like to gaze in the face of just one soul whose fellow-travelling with me. It's boring here, ahead of my own on earth.'

Yet that 'I' was no selfish I; it was the selfish with a plus sign pasted on the end. Mayakovsky wanted to be released from himself, to be released even from people like himself; to be released from the artistic role. He didn't need a middle class style therapizing help replete with sensitivity-pose, self-denial and 'concerned' paternalism, but a real ambient help inseparable from the everyday spaces of real existence. 'In the thirteenth year of the Revolution, I'm under the impression I need help...I demand help – not the gratification of non-existent virtues.'

This is the exact opposite of sacrificial militancy. But where could this help come from? Moves towards self-realisation – so inextricably and intimately connected with the momentum of revolutionary moments superseding themselves; a collective self-realisation; of highs within the lows and lows within the highs were disappearing/evaporating, as a black square of nothingness rigidly descended. Instead of Mayakovsky encountering an ever-widening circle of friends, he experienced nothing but contraction, disavowal and recurrent stabs in the back. The disaffection of friends hurt like hell and the guy expressed the feeling baldly – just the way it is - like losing limbs. On the night of his 'homemade jubilee' prepared by close comrades, a former friend who had recently attacked him moved to congratulate him. Mayakovsky turned away poignantly saying, 'No let him go away. He hasn't understood a thing. They tear me to shreds, they tear people from me with pieces of my flesh...Let him go...'

Self-absorption, self-pity? Isn't it all part of hedonism, its downside if you like? What more is to be said about hedonism? Now, in the early 1970s all around us, hedonism is declared something like a petite-bourgeois phenomenon, especially by the Althusserians. It can be, but more essentially it is part of the social process of collective self-realisation and the will to live, a rage; a desire as a revolutionary trajectory more powerful than ever it was in Mayakovsky's time. We make disruption; we make revolution for our own fulfilment and pleasure as the desire for authentic life rages ceaselessly inside our bodies. And the 'I' constantly moving and becoming must also find some kind of relation with an ever-uglier world within the orbits of uglys own alienated movement – the movement of capital. If the 'I' doesn't find that balance it flounders in illusion and the history of late 19th and early 20th century art and anarchism is littered with the dislocated 'I' –from Van Gogh to Ravachol. Certainly Mayakovsky's 'I' can be explained partly (but only partly) by the individual trajectory of the rebel which Victor Serge comments upon so well in *Men in Prison*. On his own past and that of the Bonnot Gang too, Serge says, 'We have committed great errors, comrades. We wanted to be revolutionaries, we were only rebels. We must become termites boring obstinately, patiently, all our lives: In the end the dike will crumble..... The bolts are still locked, but already I feel free, sure of myself, somewhere within me, there is a calm hatred, like a still ocean. I will turn it into strength.'

And isn't that also illusory and just so boringly part and parcel of this excuse we still call life? Mayakovsky for sure couldn't take such a dispassionate view of himself, yet we know the terrible pain that Serge went through simply by reading *Men in Prison* and *Memoirs of a Revolutionary.* Surely it was no less a pain than Mayakovsky's? However there's an essential difference: the very dynamism of the now disjointed revolt of words and syntax expressed in and through Mayakovsky imperiously demanded the world as its arena. The liberation of words demanded (equally imperiously) material realisation in everyday space and time where everything was possible. They still do.

Serge's style of presentation, though not his content is traditional; it doesn't want to be there as a living presence, as fact, in a humdrum everyday which can become superb almost in an instance. It was a form of sublimated writing whereby you were able to dull the pain and thus was very different from the terrible dilemma raging within a Mayakovsky who couldn't sublimate. On the threshold, where everything was possible, nothing was deemed possible. Inside Mayakovsky's body an emotionally insupportable future of impotent rage and endless, painful super-frustration was beginning to congeal, which in his poem, *Lenin*, attacks the cult of 'bronzing Lenin' embracing a spontaneous terrorism. 'Surely Lenin won't be mobbed: Leader of the Grace of God! / If he had been royal and divine, I wouldn't have spared myself out of rage, / I'd have pit myself against the procession line, cut across the crowd and the funeral cortege. / I'd have found enough cussing and fucking words for blasting ears, And before they could smother my cry and down me, / I'd have hurled to the heaven blasphemies, And battered the Kremlin with Bombs:- Down With.'

Yet even with the 'communist' secret police around Mayakovsky got away with this! Yet isn't this the nub that has never been brought to light: that connection between the artistic avant-garde and an explosively but necessarily disorganised 'terrorism'? (If it was organised it would lose its point); of that concrete overlap between the Impressionists, the French individualist anarchists and ESPECIALLY, the Symbolists. It was more than sympathy for each other's seemingly different paths; they, as it were, detonated each other. Yes there was a gap - though hardly amounting to a separation - for the simple reason that as the years rolled by they tended to blur and blend with each other, sucking in even the more psychotic aspects of detonation as the subconscious was more and more prized open. (One need only think of Breton's ultimate surrealist act of going into the crowd and shooting at random).

The increasingly wild rebellion of Mayakovsky's thoughts and almost uncontrollable body reactions goes - as further years rolled by –to the actuality of the Angry Brigade in the UK along with those other individuals who came out of a repetitive artistic avant-garde of the 1950s and early 1960s – and therefore because it was more or less a repeat, was experienced as that much more inauthentic – and as consequence almost ineluctably seemed to engender a detonating, quasi 'terrorist' fandango i.e. like happened to Kunzelmann of the Berlin Commune (though there were thousands of others) once the truth dawned that they weren't creative originals. But in these latter decades things generally have been getting worse and worse as social/spatial life has becoming that much more colonised, with capital invading everyday life and sucking away our very life blood. Alienation has been ever increasing, expanding its domain as life's promise of an infinite expansion of authentic possibilities narrows towards programmed, deathly perspectives. It thus became a natural reaction; a life affirming natural reaction to lash out simply to try and cast aside that fever seemingly implanted inside a head swollen with a brain pressing against a delicate cranium like a molten lump of iron. Pushed, pushed, as it were to a revolutionary suicide far more intransigent than Mayakovsky's experiment with Russian roulette, which was straightforward in comparison though typically for Mayakovsky this was a gamble with fate.

Perhaps as I've intimated, Mayakovsky's 'I' was the birth of a new kind of 'I' of a bebop-like, free form, collectively autonomous individual which this increasing hell is pregnant with. Mayakovsky came too early; he couldn't adjust that 'I' to anything like a coherent social trajectory because such a reality simply wasn't in the offing. It's easy enough to say that the isolation of the real revolutionary must not be something to be feared and that in difficult periods it must be stoically, even grimly tolerated, as, after all, populism and a general opportunism are much worse disasters; but then hell, you've only got one shot at this brief candle of life. Psychological delirium is an absolute nightmare and shit, there are many tragic instances of this conundrum in revolutionary history. Rosa Luxembourg wrote rather sensitively about this vis-à-vis the 'betrayal' of the Second International in *The Junius Pamphlet: The Crisis of German Social Democracy* saying, 'The voice of our party would have acted as a wet blanket upon the chauvinist intoxication of the masses. It would have preserved the intelligent proletariat from delirium.'

If you like Mayakovsky was poignantly aware that he was increasingly separated from his 'poetic' constituents. For, as the revolution unfolded, he deliberately altered the tone of his futurist endeavours. He tried to deploy common language within the 'verse libre' of Futurism; a process that didn't just take place overnight but slowly accelerated. Gleb Struve says, 'He deliberately vulgarised and lowered the poetic vocabulary to suit the vulgar, unrefined taste. Among his pre-revolutionary works his long poem *A Cloud in Trousers* is typical of what he is capable of, so far as the powerful poetic effects and the unmitigated vulgarity of speech and coarseness of content are concerned.'

After the revolution, using new techniques, even speaking on the radio, Mayakovsky conducted simple propaganda work which occasionally used new formal freedoms evolved through Futurism. He warned the people not to drink un-boiled water, explained the Soviet's new laws and made general 'commercial' advertisements for the state which Mayakovsky saw as an educational medium appealing to illiterates to build a new society.

Then we encounter a new contradiction! Mayakovsky's language was a very different language, it was neither 'common' nor was it the language of the so-called 'cultured' as syntax and generally acceptable meanings of words were considerably – and intentionally – creatively mangled. Neologism, as with much Futurist verse, was frequently used by Mayakovsky against the backdrop of a Russia where widespread illiteracy was perceived as a serious problem. It caused quite a problem not only for others, especially those in power, but for Mayakovsky too, Although here, one cannot go into the greater problems of language and semantics, it's enough to say that Lenin had a very narrow conception of the meaning of words – a narrow conception that has been inherited by the legion of toy Bolshevikhs. Enough to say too that the workers and peasants were meant only to learn proper sentence construction; thus the wider, evocative powers of language, the sensual language that Mayakovsky innovated / assimilated/evolved through his own originality was anathema to the conceptions of the Leninist political avant-garde. Indeed Lenin's comments upon Mayakovsky's language are banal and blinkered: 'He shouts;

invents some kind of distorted words, in fact everything about him isn't what's wanted and difficult to understand.'

But was it that difficult? Mayakovsky more and more got caught up in street argot montaged on to futurist neologism as well as consciously mimicking the jerkiness of new industrial techniques where 'workers' soviets plus electrification' seemed to herald the *promesse de bonheur*. His was a creative transition from the written to a more compelling, active spoken lifestyle; anticipation perhaps; a pre-figuring maybe of a colourful jive language jam-packed with a rich, everyday subversive flow threatening the whole empire of established discourse. Regarding future hopes, one can safely say that the liberated speech of total creative revolution will hardly be the language of academics and the diction of museum curators. That doesn't mean a future of a vague, inchoate free-for-all (although that necessarily will be in the creative mix too) but it does mean that language will acquire new and strange ways of communications, more upfront, less prone to deceit, manipulation and lies. For certain that if the revolution discriminates against the historical becoming of such a new language it will discriminate against the essence of the revolution itself; in short a 'revolution' not worth preserving.

As for myself, I hope to re-find the vernacular of Co Durham pitching it at higher levels; to rid myself of the deadening niceties that have been imposed upon me by academia; in short to resolve my language dyslexia (a schizophrenic mix of the illiterate and the high flown) in a richer social becoming.

As for Mayakovsky he certainly wanted to realise his transitional free verse in the poetic impulses of the masses. Deploying their language was one bridge to the future; another was by directly speaking to them without intermediaries, whilst yet another was becoming a chaotic tribune of the people – if that doesn't sound too corny. Mayakovsky actually did go from town to town and from village to village, from factory to tank, to warship to... whatever and wherever, forever trying to slough off the typical artistic, cultural venue. He tried 'to know', to speak to the people through trying to realise himself as a new troubadour of revolution; therefore not really a traditional tribune at all but one who was also out for a good time; somebody who helped enlighten in a more rounded, dialectical sense, listening as well as propagandising: 'When you got up with bullets and lay down with a gun, / where your breath merged with the masses own breath / with such a hand you march to life again, / to rejoicings, to work and to death.'

But doesn't this also have something which smacks of dishonesty too? Mayakovsky certainly wasn't part of the Russian Civil War embattled proletariat. Much of such 'identification' was more to do with wish fulfilment as he certainly was never in the thick of any fighting as Victor Serge undoubtedly was. It could be said that Mayakovsky's visceral need for real contact meant he tended to move in all directions at once, even in unprincipled directions like joining RAPP, the Stalinist Revolutionary Association of Writers. According to Victor Shklovsky, Mayakovsky participated in order 'to get closer to his workers' auditoriums' only to fall into a 'dead sea, surrounded on all sides by interdictions and citations.'

In fact all of Mayakovsky's attempts, notwithstanding the attempt, to get into 'contact' with the '150 million' of the masses amounted to little more than utter rubbish. For what really excites us today are Mayakovsky's regular incitements to something amounting to ubiquitous vandalism amongst all his pretensions to 'good works'. And it seems this excellent, attractive posture has been politely forgotten or pushed to one side by all today's legions of 'socialist' poets/cretinous artists and aspiring cultural bureaucrats who wish to lead (ugh) the 'cultural' side of the 'new' revolution.

Moreover, increasingly Mayakovsky dropped his posturings and pretences as he increasingly withdrew from the boisterous presentation of an ego that was beginning to disintegrate. It could be said he was finally encountering the authentic the more the mask slipped; going in search of love and beginning to speak in lyrical, sweet tones without ever abandoning the revolution where 'the love boat of life has crashed on philistine reefs'. This latter line from Mayakovsky's poem/anguished tirade, *About This,* wasn't mentioned or written about for a full twenty years after publication. It was a statement where love and the revolution fuse with each other – 'lyrics we've attached with repeated bayonet digs' - though finally it was the obverse which happened: the lyrical turned against him hurting more than ever a bayonet thrust could. In his suicide note, Mayakovsky said, 'love has wounded me forever'. What and for whom was that unrequited love? It seems on the surface to be a general comment on society at large; the failure of a revolutionary erotic ambience to materialise. And for sure that's all true but in *About This* Mayakovsky seems to be also commiserating with the young communist leaguer who wants to jump off a bridge into the river Neva. Now we also know that this was a metaphor for his own erotic failure, indeed the catastrophic failure of his own personal relationships. For years he openly (?) had loved Lily Brik, wife of Osip Brik, the rich patron of the Futurists. This love seemed unrequited. Desperately, Mayakovsky had looked for others, finally (I reckon) to fall in love with Lily's sister, Elsa who lived in Paris and had married a French cavalry officer. Alas, that too like a 'destiny of libido' (Freud) quickly involved rejection, and beyond that lay delirium. Later Elsa Triolet divorced the cavalry officer and went on later to marry a surrealist who was to become an arch French Stalinist, Louis Aragon, well after the latter's great creative days re the *Paysan du Paris* and *Traite du Style*, etchad gone forever.

   I would finally suggest that Stalin basically had taken everything away from Mayakovsky; adding insult to injury by deliberately canonizing him but only in the knowledge the guy was well and truly dead and buried. In *The First Circle* decades later, Sholzenhitsyn disdainfully recounts how in his particular gulag prison a book of Mayakovsky's writings (probably by then obligatory reading by a Stalinised state) was used in the oppressive summer heat to keep a broken window open. It was as though on every level Mayakovsky had been brutally check-

mated, cynically dispatched to oblivion by myriad sleights of hand......
David Wise 1972

On Tatlin: The Great Fool...

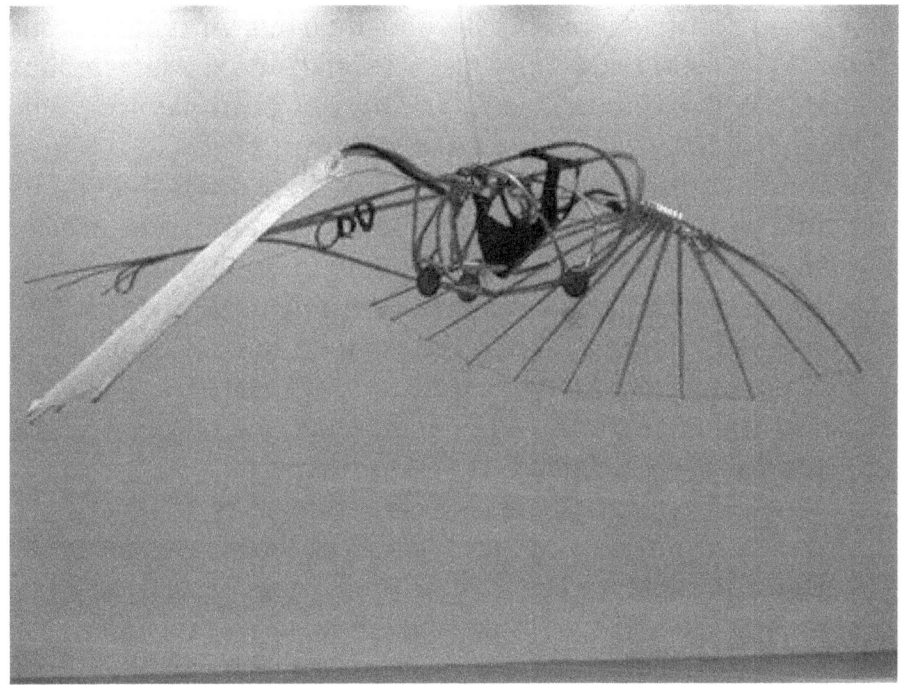

Vladimir Tatlin's *Le-Tatlin* / Ornithopter
Photo of Tatlin by the German Dadaist, Raoul Hausmann

Vladimir Tatlin's aim was to put cubist space into a three dimensional lived form. It's all kind of old hat now for us at the end of the era of modernity we have found desperately wanting and empty. Ehrenburg said that the Café Pittoresesque, where Tatlin along with others of the Russian avant-garde displayed more than their wares was 'the only café that all the artistic sewers in Europe's capitals would envy', as, after all, Tatlin in collaboration with El Lissitsky, had fundamentally altered its interior. From then on Tatlin wanted to spatially recreate the world......

On the one hand, Tatlin is seen as the most modern of the moderns of the first 50 years or so of the 20th century yet the first written re-appraisal of Tatlin in Russian didn't come about until 1966, thirteen years after his death! On the other hand the guy was in person a somewhat yob of a guy from the back of beyond, of an old peasant Russia, which was rapidly dying out, and as he got older he seemed more and more to cling to this past. Then, Tatlin shared his sleeping quarters with his famous *Tower* (*Monument to the Third International*) and the less famous *Glider*, (*The Ornithopter*), sadly taking refuge in painting. The German Dadaist, George Grosz, said of him:

> 'I met Tatlin the great fool once again. He was living in a small, ancient and decrepit apartment. Some of the hens he kept slept on his bed. In a corner they laid eggs.....behind him a mattress, entirely consumed by rust was leaning against the wall; on it sat a couple of sleeping hens, their heads in their feathers. This was the good Tatlin's frame and when he played his homemade balalaika – it was growing dark already outside the uncurtained window, the panes of which had been replaced by small plates of wood – he gave the impression not of an ultra-modern constructivist, but a piece of the genuine, ancient Russia, as if from a book by Gogol; and there was suddenly a melancholy humour in the room.'

Tatlin may have died forgotten but in the early 1920s he was regarded as one of the leading Russian artistic revolutionaries. Nay, more than that, he was a kind of innovative cultural boss sitting astride the new hierarchy. I think it's this moment which makes Tatlin's example so appealing to so many younger so-called revolutionaries today: gauchiste artists who in their baneful dreams would like to take over culturally bankrupt institutions and become new 'enlightened' bureaucrats and powerful careerists of creativity! (Ugh) After all, Tatlin was elected leader of all artistic organisations in Moscow. He was head of the Narkompros Board for Plastic Art and Head of the Dept of Painting at the Free Studies School in Moscow. He was commissioned by the Commissariat of Education under Lunarcharsky to make the *Monument to the Third International (the Tower)* and which has become the most famous of the Russian avant-garde constructions. Many copies have been made. Perhaps the most notable is by Ulf Linde in Utrecht and another stands (painted red) in the forecourt of the Management Studies building of the Central London Polytechnic. As a symbol, it is the insignia of New Left Books. Yet as a monument does it really have much relevance for us today? Like shite it does.

As with many others involved in the Russian avant-garde, Tatlin wanted to grasp the whole of space again by a kind of unity of the arts through the use of new materials – his famous 'culture of materials'. He intuitively - more than theoretically or through historical knowledge – realised that all the central reference points in the arts had been lost and the only way out of this impasse, this avoidable crisis for Tatlin, was through a huge extension of formal, modernistic, machine-made radicalism applied to the everyday utilitarian objects we make use of, which should become charged adjuncts of a changed revolutionary lifestyle. It went little deeper than that, for if he'd looked behind surface appearance, Tatlin would have realised the revolution had soured pretty quickly and that we should have been preparing for a really subversive new revolution! Instead he accepted the shibboleths. In a manifesto Tatlin wrote in 1920 apropos of the *Monument to the Third International* he says, 'The results of this are models which stimulate us to inventions in our works of creating a new world and which call upon the producers to exercise control over the forms encountered in our everyday life.'

What new world, what changed everyday life? Hopes yes, but precious little realisation. The Third International had become threadbare; the Kronstadt sailors' revolt was only a year away, and an ultra-leftist, anti-Bolshevikh communism well on the rise around the corpse of Rosa Luxembourg, and yet it seems that Tatlin's ears were closed to all this! Moreover, about the only familiar and human detail in the monument is the canteen, as basically *The Tower* is a representation of vulgarised communism assisted by a crude technolatry, or should I also add, a technology which has little to do with any liberating practical science like say as Brunel had practised e.g. his improvisations when constructing the Great Western Railway.

If you like, Tatlin's is an aestheticised technology based on the synthesis of architecture and the leftovers of sculpture and painting that had been in a purposeful, creative freefall. Tatlin had said the artist's 'creative method is qualitatively different from that of an engineer'. In reality, the tower's dynamic central spiral is similar to that of the *Bottle in Space* by the Italian Futurist Boccioni. I think this comparison is better than the usual one, that of the Eiffel Tower in Paris, though I think there's little point in researching the iconography of the Tower. Trotsky in, *Literature and Revolution,* had also compared the *Monument to the Third International* to the Eiffel Tower. He said of the latter, 'It stimulates us by the technical simplicity of its forms but it alienates us by its purposelessness;. (The International Lettrist, Chetchglov in the 1950s, plammed to blow the Eiffel Tower up; an early indication of a drift into tachiste spontaneous 'terrorism'; harbinger of the Angry Brigade and an argument elaborated in, *A Catastrophic Social / Creative Impasse (....by way of the personal tragedy of Mayakovsky).*

Nonetheless, Tatlin subscribed to a utilitarian ideology that for the life of him he could never adhere to as always the poetic and evocative was attempting a takeover within the depth of his being. In one of his final brochures, *The Man on the Stage*, a photo displays bent discs hanging from the ceiling which when illuminated, evoke the moon, like something out of Elizabethan poetry in Shakespeare's time. Indeed Shklovsky called Tatlin's utilitarianism 'a strange utilitarianism'. Trotsky was more than in agreement, seeing little that was utilitarian in *the Tower*. Somehow you get the impression of scaffolding that the builders have forgotten to take away. In any case why should revolutionary meetings take place in cylinders and cones amidst all the debris of Cézanne and Picasso? Trotsky's critique remains on the level of the visual and goes no deeper; now we must more than plummet greater critical depths; we must again practically act upon our conclusions.

The Ornithopter (the glider) was also called *Le-Tatlin:* a Russian futurist neologism meaning to fly. Many contemporary commentators immediately invoked the experiments of Leonardo and Lilienthal. Tatlin himself mentioned that Icarus was the first to fly. Again, this is a big harking back spliced onto an aesthetic technology at once. As Zelinsky said, humdrum 'home handicraft' and / or 'technological Khlebnikovism'. As for myself I can look at *the Ornithopter* as a bizarre piece of Art Nouveau. Moreover, science, apart from spontaneous science, is of little avail here. Tatlin was far too much the primitive, watchful, old fashioned peasant for that and for inspiration he simply watched the flight of bees in meadows, although some commentators have rather pointlessly tried to make some connection between the pioneer of Russian rocket research, K. E. Tsiolkovsky who in 1912 had said, 'if the aeroplane is ever to be replaced by ornithopters, then rational planning of the latter will demand an even more thorough study of birds and insects ability to fly.' I doubt if Tatlin ever read Tsiolkovsky. In any case, it was Tatlin's belief that the machine could be propelled by muscular power alone and was therefore quite at odds with Tsiolkovsky. Tatlin himself said of the glider, 'I have made it as an artist...don't you think *Le Tatlin* gives an impression of aesthetic perfection, like a hovering seagull?' This is early ecological stuff and what's even more interesting, Tatlin then went on to say, 'I want also to give back to man the feeling of flight. We have been robbed of this by the mechanical flight of the aeroplane'. I also like to think it's more than that, more to do with a multi-dimensional world and the insights of various mystics. That sensation of flight that goes back to ancient religious sects, to the witches on fly agaric and the shamans; all a far cry from the Age of Enlightenment.

So often the Tower and the later Ornithopter are regarded as early examples of aestheticized objects (objet d'art?) which began to bridge the gap between art and modern technology. Perhaps, but hasn't this trajectory since Tatlin only had baneful conclusions, resulting in a plethora of spectacles and ludicrous constructs like the recent displays of the idiotic Nicholas Schoeffer's light towers he refers to as Cybernetic Serendipity; or on an even more banal level, the pseudo technical / industrial apologetics of the Art Placement Group. (In any case how can you make the baneful social control inherent in cybernetics become playful serendipity?)

None of these pathetic, so-called experiments ever once question the traditional role of the artist and the omnipotent sway of now bankrupt art objects have today over our lives. Do we need a 'new' aesthetics or, do we dispense with aesthetics altogether? It seems that the only aesthetic question that has any relevance today is, 'How much does it cost?' True there must be a creative technology but then creativity and aesthetics are no longer synonymous; in fact they are poles apart. The useless pursuit of a fusion between art and technology is nothing but a reification avoiding the question of how technology can become genuinely creative and relevant once a total social revolution reaches a stage of no going back. At that moment technology, for the first time in world history especially, will do most of the work that the wage labourers of today have no choice but to do; not as is the case in the present organisation of society, with the increasing organic composition of capitalism defraying some of the costs of variable capital (wages). Indeed some of the Russian avant-garde vaguely intuited some such future scenario. El Lissitsky, surprisingly, considering his often baneful pre-figuration of something like a Russian MacLuhanism, said, 'Communism will have to be left behind because Suprematism which embraces the totality of life's phenomena – will attract everyone away from the domination of work.'

Although not really elaborated – it's not much more than

a vague intuition – it is a remarkable enough forecast. The best I think that can be said about Tatlin's experiments were that despite heading for a cul-de-sac there was something interestingly mock heroic about them; they were attempts to bring about radical, fundamental changes before the wider perspectives and possible subsequent problems had been thought through. There is of course, no point in even attempting to repeat them. It could be said that the Tower reveals Tatlin's bourgeois cum bureaucratic conceptions re the functioning of a transitional *'proletarian'* democracy, ('proletarian' deliberately italicised because the proletariat must, of course, abolish itself through a successful uprising). Tatlin in his construction envisages a separation between executive and legislative to be housed in distinct cones or cylinders and thus (whether the guy was conscious of this or not) a feature of bourgeois state rule. All previous experiments in transitional proletarian democracy, such as the Paris Commune of 1871 and the 1905 revolution in Russia, had seen a fusion; a possible supercession of the legislative, executive and judicial with no supposedly neutral civil service proclaiming declarations and distributing / enforcing enactments etc. In the 1905 uprising we saw for the first time in world history, the creation of workers' councils where delegates were elected from work places on permanent revocable mandates: in short, tendentially creating the most advanced form of democracy (direct democracy) the world has ever seen. Most revolutions since then have tended to throw up similar forms of proletarian, self-management, including Hungary 1956 and to a lesser extent May 1968 in France (though the French Communist party managed to stymie or derail much self-organisation in the factories).

But where is all the earlier experience of direct democracy in Tatlin's Tower. Well it ain't there folks because this is for The Party and nothing but the Party Line! In fact it falls in line with the Bolshevikh dictatorship (the baneful Workers' State) over the autonomous power of the Workers' Councils. Let's face it. the guy was ignorant regarding a lot of basics. On the general level

Tatlin was submissive, at best naively following all the changes in the Bolshevikh party line. At worst, his *Art into Technology Manifesto* is prefaced by a singularly stupid comment of Stalin's, 'During the epoch of construction, technology determines everything.'

As for the future will we need such Internationals housed in such monuments? Come off it, of course not! Assemblies, Workers' Councils (call them what you will) will meet anywhere and everywhere: a university building, a factory, a mill, a warehouse, a football stadium, a concert hall, a cinema – which buildings are appropriated won't be of any consequence because these structures will also be in the process of losing their former roles, never, hopefully, to return to their original purpose. In any case such popular ferment will contain within itself radical critique of all monumentality and all the edifices of state functions etc. as well as the ubiquitous application of all the stylistic 'innovations' of modern art nowadays applied to vast stretches of our urban spaces, especially our living areas. Inevitably too, consciously or not, there will be a critique in motion of all modernist processes not only elaborated by Tatlin, Malevich, Lissitsky and others but for us in the West omnipotently imposed by all the fallouts from the Bauhaus to De Stijl, especially the sheer brutality of the International Style as moulded by the horrors of Le Corbusier etc. And, let's face it, the Russians tended to back all this crap to the hilt. In one of his letters from the Unovis School in Vitebsk, Malevich ended with the salutation, 'Greetings to non-objective Holland and all the innovators living there.' For let's be honest, the difference between Russian applications of modern art to most aspects of design – supposedly 'communist' in orientation – differed little from what was taking place in the West; a little bit more bizarre perhaps (e.g. Malevich's crockery) but not fundamentally that different (e.g. the Dutchman's, Rietveld's nutty De Stijl chair and both meant to be utilitarian objects that are profoundly non-utilitarian). Even today, a blinkered leftist will always persist in coming out with the notion that the Bauhaus was better once the Communist Party apparatchik Hannes Meyer took over from the social democratic Walter Gropius.

Anyway, within the context of contemporary advanced Workers' Councils, once the repressive state apparatus has been subdued and conquered, immediate tasks - no matter what – regarding the exigencies of the urban situation will still, first and foremost have to deal with the immediate socialisation of the land and the abolition of rents and mortgages etc; meaning that an active critique of modern art and design will come about somewhat farther down the scale of urgent tasks. In any case such critique is more likely to happen spontaneously, outside of any solemn decrees from on high (no matter that it is from some top dog workers' council) and happen it will and quickly simply because the proletariat has been at the drastic receiving end of a modern art funnelled through design, especially an architecture degree zero and will be only too delighted to critique its miserable presence in a probably almost endless, mass active alteration and supercession, particularly an urbanism built around car transport.

At that point the pathetic notion of the 'philistine workers' in comparison to the 'enlightened intellectuals' will well and truly have bitten the dust. Of course it isn't (and never was) as cut and dried as that; and whilst recognising that many Russian 'workers' laughed at the Tower, unfortunately preferring traditional sculptural busts of Karl Marx and at some moments thoroughly objected to Mayakovsky's free verse. Elsewhere this was not so, particularly in Italy. Gramsci mentions that even before the First World War the radical workers of Milan and Turin supported Italian Futurism and that three quarters of the copies sold of the futurist periodical *Lacerba* were bought by them.

More to the point, it hasn't been easy to supersede the perspective of an interlocking art / technology / new architecture syndrome. The project of the total work of art was there well before the Constructivists, especially throughout the latter half of the 19th century with John Ruskin, William

Morris's Arts & Crafts, Art Nouveau and even the Pre-Raphaelites. Since the closing of the Bauhaus in the early 1950s we have had the New Bauhaus which, though rather more subversive (capitalism was at least regarded as the enemy), fell within the same paradigms of the grande projet – a slowly disintegrating Le Corbusier-ism – whereby the designs of seemingly liberated individuals would, from on top, help liberate the people living in this new habitation of movable spaces made of ultra-modern, manufactured, pliable, lighter materials. But who wants these on top enlightened supermen liberating us? Why cannot we free ourselves in a wonderment of different ways - neither modern nor ancient - and collectively remake our own spaces from the bottom up minus the guidance of the grande projet? Let there be the abolition of money among wildness, wilderness ..... and sanitation.

'Revolution is the Festival of the Oppressed' Or is it and in what way? I am still of the opinion that the festivals remain the most relevant moments of an almost neo-artistic situation in post revolutionary Russia, though almost in this context still had miles to go. Most of these festivals were directed by artists and in fact grew out of the theatre through experimental individuals like Evreinov, Eisenstein, Pudovkin and even Mayakovsky. Because of this imposition these festivals weren't therefore examples of spontaneous festivity and nowhere near as organic to a restless urban population as say the jazz festivals and cutting contests redolent of New Orleans, For instance Storyville was around at the same time; even earlier. Moreover, some of the Russian events were really very tightly organised, particularly the staged repeats of aspects of the October 1917 'revolution' (some, more accurately, would say Bolshevikh coup d'etat). Most of this street staging was meant to celebrate 'communism' and the factory and the Noise Orchestra directive in *The Concert of Factory Sirens and Steam Whistles* (see the *Icteric* mag) correspond to the period of 'war time communism', especially the emphasis on electrification following Lenin's famous call for 'Soviets plus electrification'. I think these celebrations were deliberately manipulated by a prevailing technolatry and consequence of this was they were not by any means anonymous events allowing for a democratic, leaderless, spontaneity. Most were due to the initiative of two poets, Gaster and Mayakovsky. According to Fuelop Mueller, 'They pointed out that proletarian music should no longer be confined to a narrow room, but that its audience should be the population of the whole district. The factory whistle was in their opinion, to be adapted to be the new and predominant orchestral instrument, for its tone could be heard by whole quarters and remind the proletariat of its real home, the factory.' Jeez, and what a middle class assumption; only somebody who'd never been in a factory day in day out could come out with such bilge. As for a factory whistle remember on a clear night a decade or so before these Russian spectacles, Buddy Bolden's horn could be heard twelve miles away in the alligator swamps of the Mississippi delta!

Let's cut the crap; I think this was more the bald truth of the matter. A few decades later and things have been given the gloss of rose-tinted spectacles. By 1966 a Russian critic name of Mayeov (?) in a periodical called *ISSKUSTVO* seems to reflect, to impose ideas emanating from contemporary France and which are probably well wide of the mark. Of these staged festivals he says, 'They are a living intercourse between human beings, unrestricted by objects or hierarchic structures. [You what?] Its specific feature is play, self-realisation, without which no one truly exists.' …… and, 'Unlike art, which in its aims is equally ideal, the festival realises in a more active manner the aesthetic transformation of reality'. because 'in this festive union of the people, man is liberated from considerations and obligations', for in, 'The principle of play, action is the antithesis of watching, it supports the tendency to eliminate all difference between actor and spectator'.

Fine words, but they don't remotely describe what was taking place on the ground; a leftist recuperation, a distortion, even a lie, because the masses in these Russian spectacles hardly ever acted spontaneously but were organised by the Artist /

Director. True, the better, more honest artistic directors at this moment in Russia did tend to see something of their contradictory position merely hoping they could help facilitate the self-realisation of the masses. Finally even Mayeov comes back down to earth recognising that the ideal of the festival is to include all the people in "common brotherhood" but this is only possible when all "barriers of property, class, culture separating people have been abolished and this ideal can only be achieved in communism." (Interestingly the abolition of money or wage labour isn't mentioned here).

The Russian festivals remained situated at the junction between art and life; the festival becoming the mediating event or moment between the two separated plains of art and life. They remained contradictory: the alienated watching, spectacular element remaining mixed with an active participation which, in reality was nothing more than pseudo participation because programmed. Thus, these so-called festivals weren't really genuine festivals at all (in the mass subversive sense we now recognise by the description) but really extensions; a loosening maybe of a generally rigid Bolshevised monumentality. Most certainly they can't be seen as a pre-figuration of tomorrow's genuinely revolutionary festivals, inseparable from subversive uprising. They have been pre-figured in the recent ghetto insurrections in American cities and even the sub-cultural expressions of collective juvenile delinquency from the 1950s onwards. Moreover, before that there were also many moments of ritual mass celebration that completely altered their character and got out of hand. Take for instance that suppressed but notable incident on the eve of armistice in 1945 when the drunken crowds in Trafalgar Square took to mass copulation, so an alienated festival thus acquired a sudden sensual authenticity, a realisation, if you like, of Hegel's curlicue, 'The true is a moment of the false.'

This was play in the widest definition of an evolving sense of play is and it could be said that such play has been there lurking in the background for millennia. The difference is this that evolving definition has acquired an urgency of realisation which must become the dominant thrust in society starting right now by collectively and imaginatively subverting the miserable conditions of modern capitalism as collectively we create the conditions for a new world. Inevitably we will immediately encounter all the forces of the old order out there to stop this happening and who will deploy all their police units and their vast techniques of subtle conditioning and deadly persuasion. Once, it was said, 'The church used to burn those whom it called sorcerers in order to repress the primitive tendencies to play preserved in popular festivals. In the society that is at present dominant which mass produces wretched pseudo games (Isle of Wight pop concerts etc) devoid of participation, any true activity is necessarily classified as criminal. It remains semi-clandestine and comes to life as scandal.' (From an anonymous leaflet).

In a sense it could be said there is something of a link between the modern day Isle of Wight pseudo-festivals and the earlier Russian, stage managed events in the deployment of a common pseudo participation which passes itself off as real. The most we can say is that these festivals (and there are more and more of them) have finally at least given rise to very deep insights into the nature of authentic festivity as opposed to a reified dancing-like passivity (the seeming spontaneous movement of the spectators) and it's a concept that has now become central to all genuine revolutionary theory and practice.

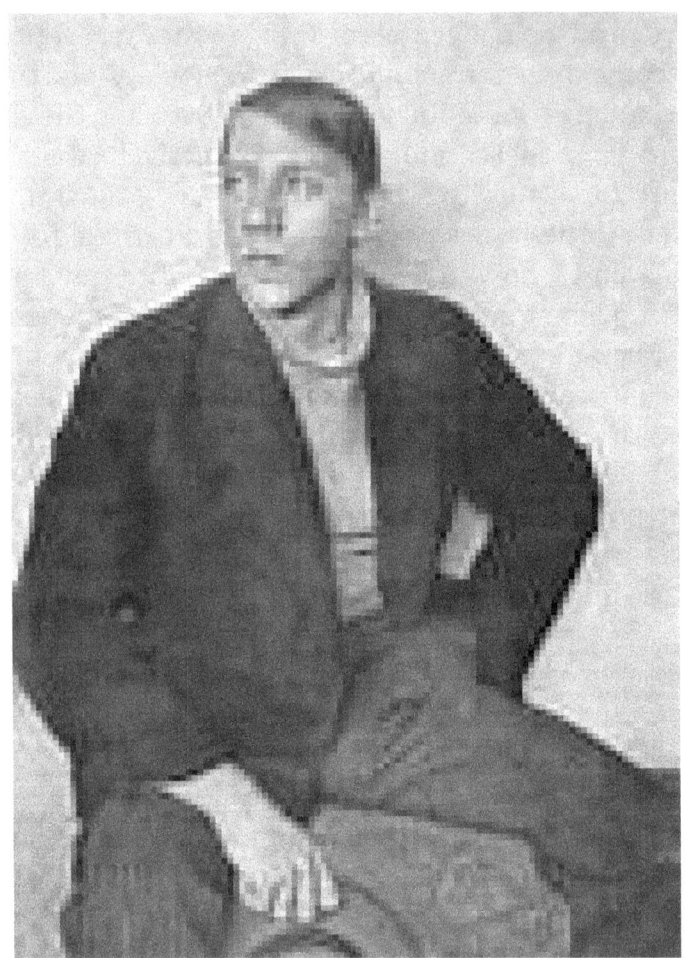

11 - RALPH RUMNEY

*From Artist to Situationist
and Back Again*

Dave Wise
2007

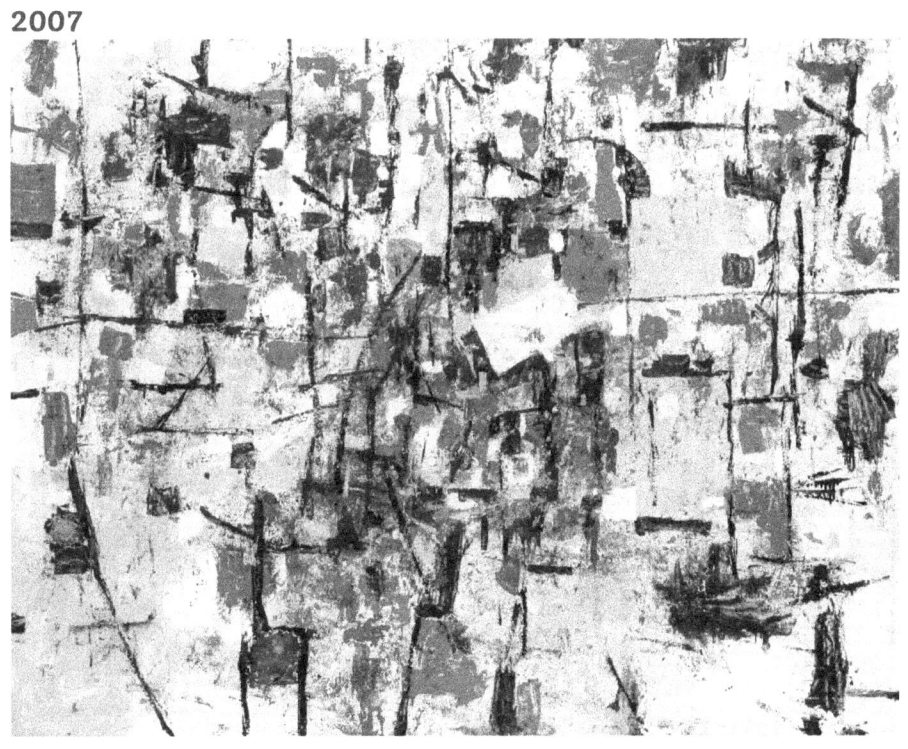

Ralph Rumney was a co-founder of the International Situationists in 1957. Originally from the north of England he was an artist who tried to move beyond the boundaries of art; one encompassing a profounder social vision helping initiate psychogeography and the practise of the derive. Failing in his quest he fell back on prior artistic paradigms venturing into the circles of a cultural high society forever tending to gave him short shrift.

Let's first consider Ralph Rumney's excellent points: In his mid teens in the early 1950s he tried to get hold of copies of De Sade's books, which created violent contra-temps with his parson father. He then courageously refused the compulsory National Service stint in the army. Going on the run he was forced to appear in a Bristol court where he gave a spirited, existential, even Camus-like defence of his refusal when it would have been much easier to have fallen back on a more conservative, 'thou shalt not kill' religious plea-bargaining.

Not too afraid of the consequences he had the courage to face penury with equanimity: 'I discovered material poverty at the same time as intellectual wealth'. His undoubted lust for life meant he could take on board a more or less youthful street existence for a while in London and Paris; an experience which obviously helped enormously in opening up his mind. Rumney's lifestyle was thus inseparable from developing concepts, which later were to produce the more fully worked out derive. It meant too he came slap bang up against the modernisers, the city developers and planners and he had the guts to confront them head on. Rumney hated Colin Buchanan, the chief architect responsible for the 1950s London clearances and had the honour of being excluded from the so-called radical Independents Group for condemning the architects in their midst. (No doubt this was the Smithsons and others belonging to the school of *brutalism*). Against the 'flattened universe' of modernism, Rumney's alternatives for London, though hardly fleshed-out weren't bad at all, envisaging a psychogeography of pedestrian zones (down with the car) bringing out the ambiences of the different huddled together villages that make up London.

Despite all the excellent contrariness, Rumney, no matter what, was always an artist, even in his most rebellious early days. By 1953 and only twenty years old he had landed a paid-up contract with London's Redfern Gallery and over 25 years later, not having moved on, he was teaching art at Canterbury School of Art. Throughout the years from the early 1950s onwards, exhibition after exhibition of his works followed in England, Italy and Belgium etc. Thus totality – which for people like us implies the attempted praxis of total revolution – became for Ralph Rumney 'the total praxis of art' in a re-vamped Renaissance, Italian city state sense where the artist strutting his/her stuff on the stage overshadows and overawes the paymaster: The Modern Prince. Concepts like detournement were deployed in the narrow, artistic sense of collage and montage and Rumney's substitute attack on art was against 'artism', that endless repetition of marketable themes. It became a get-out clause; a means whereby the guy didn't have to confront his artistic role. Half measures were it seems enough! All these foibles are today entirely familiar and in fits and starts deployed by all the rag-tag post-modernists *far, far, far* more mediocre than Rumney. We need only think of Tracy Emin, the Chapman Bros and Banksy…

So much for a brief historical, critical context. What follows are some thoughts on Ralph Rumney I've mulled over in my head for many a year. He's a guy who wasn't to be one thing or another, who searched but hardly found, who fell back on past historical roles (the bohemian artist) but was unable to really cut through into anything like a fully-fledged revolutionary critique – one that superseded art – and thus offering hope for the future of human kind. He seemed unsure of what he did find, like the outcome of certain derives he initiated, the best concerning east London (Limehouse) and the worst concerning Italy, (Venice).

Hesitating, unable to complete and to make ruthless but necessary jumps, Ralph fell backwards, only to then many years later update himself, revisiting somewhat his lapsed past. He merely mimicked original situationist anger as the done thing to do, a substitute anger he hoped would give him some historical presence the more he realised he was acquiring fame. There was however nothing original on offer since he'd been evicted (rightly) from the early moments of the Situationist International. This may sound harsh but there's no way Ralph Rumney achieved the clarity, audacity and heights of a Patrick Cheval, a Sebastiani or a Rene Riesel and all those *largely unknown others* who proved to be so effective in the late 1960s...and having started like this does not mean the following is *a paean of praise* for the Situationist International.

Rumney came from the same neck of the woods as my twin brother and myself and where we spent a big part of our childhood and early teens. One huge and shattering difference between Rumney and ourselves is that: Ralph didn't really *like* the north of England; we loved it and still do. Having been forced out of the Bradford/Halifax arena in the mid 1950s Rumney was *never* to return spending the rest of his life in either Italy (Venice) or southern France with a few late*ish* interludes in the most supine, traditional enclaves of a time past, typical southern English rural retreat. Rumney had called Halifax: 'A town without culture' meaning a philistine place in a pejorative sense, and try as I might to see this description indicating the beyond of culture, I obviously cannot! None the less the town that had forced him into exile put on a exhibition of their rehabilitated son in 2002.

Escaping the wrath of his father and giving a forefinger up to the family and church, he escaped – for the time – into 'revolutionary' Halifax asking the innovative but then largely unknown social historian EP Thompson to give him a bed for more than a few nights. Malcolm Imrie said in Rumney's *Guardian* obituary (March 8th 2002) that staying with EP 'deepened his understanding of Marxism' though finally I've got my doubts about that.

How did Rumney know about EP Thompson, was it through the Communist party and its youth league which he was a member of? Rumney had helped picket the army-recruiting centre in Bradford demonstrating against National Service and did he casually meet Thompson at one of these events, or what? That we'll never know! But let's imagine: Thompson at the time was re-evaluating the history of the English working classes, though his classic book on the subject was yet to be published. His research though was assisted by on-the-spot evening class tuition via the Workers' Educational Association, itself product of a form of social democratic inclusiveness. In a way, Thompson was a well-meaning toff – one of the very best of them – his students' lowly, mainly manual workers who wanted to broaden their minds. The times though were opening up and things weren't what they used to be. The workers were talking back! Thompson was telling the workers *their* history through his assiduous, remarkable and painstaking researches. For sure his worker students would listen but then they'd query and query and query. Thompson responded, acutely listening in turn and a dialectical process unfolded, just as it should. Perspectives morphed getting subtler, getting profound.

For Rumney, enforced, alienated labour wasn't something that was to figure in his life. In fact it seems he had only one typical humdrum job in his life and that was as in telephone operator in 1968 when destitute in London after he escaped from Peggy Guggenheim's private security agents in Italy and France who were trying to pin on him the blame for her daughter's suicide (Pegeen Guggenheim was Rumney's wife), After 1970, Rumney was to become a broadcaster on the French radio station ORTF, a cadre role and the type of bullshit Rumney felt more at home with.

In the age of the aesthetic economy the common thread is the redundancy of artistic form coupled with the redundancy of all the tons of empty prattle related to it and Rumney really did believe in art. In *Le Consul*, the interview-like book about certain aspects of his life, he says: 'Art once played a real role in society, and I thought it might be possible to reproduce that situation. In 1962, Debord didn't believe that at all. He was wrong I think.' No, Debord was utterly right.

Money though is quite a different matter and that's what the prattle essentially relates to; the massive wall of fictive capital, which imperiously must find an outlet in order to further enrich its self-consuming cancerous growth. Ralph gained a reputation that grew daily because of his previous association with the Situationist International, the more his 'artistic' abominations were churned out, ever increasing in value dollar-wise.

The problem with Ralph Rumney was that he couldn't make any clear break between the artistic past and the more visionary side of himself. Sad to say he could never get away from his mistakes; indeed he constantly returned to them pointing to that profoundly blocked dialectic strangling our times. Even his excellent, borrowed insight: 'the map in not the territory' was constantly revisited as art in the studio rather than a signpost on the hoped-for road leading to a passionate, vibrant, renewed daily life.

Ah yes, De Quincey! By the time Rumney hit early to mid 1950s London, De Quincey's central London rookeries around Tottenham Court Rd and Clerkenwell etc had all been well and truly cleared out, not to say completely neutered, replaced with a dull respectability. You had to go east to find anything that remotely approximated and Limehouse beckoned, still retaining something of its 19th century character, though obviously far removed from the ambiences De Quincey had experienced. Limehouse was lined with terraced housing for those streets that had been lucky enough not to have been bombed by the Luftwaffe even though the houses were often cold and damp with wet cellars prey to the effects of the river and its constant fogs. (Rumney reckons he coined the 1950s phrase: 'London destroyed more by developers than the Luftwaffe'). A Chinese community existed there with more than the occasional opium den still hanging on though by then an emerging consumer market meant opening a Chinese restaurant offered a more lucrative future. Some quickly acquired chic status serving a growing number of artistic bohemians, having chosen the area for its charm plus a nascent gay community then still criminalised. Both were attracted by cheap rents.

The area also became a magnet for the changing face of London's gangland also fascinated by its informal atmosphere and the pub, the Prospect of Whitby became a hang-out as emerging Carry On film stars like Barbara Windsor (later governess of EastEnders' Queen Vic) hooked up with that vicious sadist Ronnie Knight (later exiled to the Costa del Crime in southern Spain) who started to glamourise the pub's name as Royalty in the name of Princess Margaret and Lord Snowdon tarried with rough trade roles that Knight's crew obligingly deferred to.

Ralph Rumney was a handsome man. He had a passion for Michele Bernstein, the erstwhile, married companion of Guy Debord. The couple had an open relationship though as far as I know nothing in the early days of the Situationist International ever happened between Ralph and Michele in a sexual sense. Not that such tittle-tattle matters but deeper impulses do. Guy and Michele broke up around 1970.

Then there was another night sometimes in the early 1980s and I was talking with Michel Prigent and Lucy Forsyth about Guy Debord. Michel back then worshipped the guy (excuse the pun); a worship no matter whom or what it concerned, I've always found *impossible* to understand, seeing I'd never worshipped anybody or anything though profoundly respectful of those deserving of respect. Michel was talking about Rumney and Ms Bernstein. Debord had just told Michel how he'd thrown both of them out and what he had to say was rather different –and I think more accurate – than what has subsequently appeared in books e.g. Andrew Hussey's, The Game of War. It seems Ralph Rumney had suggested to Guy he must be in the pay of the police in order to live out his the subversive lifestyle, and if he was paying them off could he help get him some official residents' documents? Debord rightly went berserk and had shown them the door. By then it seems Rumney had decided to 'return' to revolution after a long, long absence. He thus re-invented himself donning a somewhat militant image proclaiming he was under threat from the police for being a dangerous man with dangerous views. Nothing could have been further from the truth and Ralph's dangerous phase was well and truly in the past. As we well know, he ventured to say: 'The police know who the real revolutionaries are, obviously they have to, it's their job'. But do they? Anybody who's been in any kind of trouble with the police relating to revolutionary theory and action knows Plod is pretty slow, even dumb regarding these matters.

Though I nodded, this tale was passed over with mild interest but then, almost as an afterthought, Michel laconically said – as if it was of little importance - that Michele Bernstein just before they broke up, asked Guy to whip her. Michel looked mildly perplexed and said Debord couldn't do it and that was that. It was mentioned as a casual fact; a comment without theory as to the whys and wherefores and yes, maybe it wasn't worthy of further elaboration.

None the less my mind raced. Why? To me it was now symptomatic of a maimed, imperious, genitalised impulse having tipped over from the essence of the expected beautiful social liberation, inseparable from the totality of liberation having utterly lost its way, even capsizing. The walls of the late 1960s were full of transcendental longings like: 'You say you love me. Oh say it with paving stones' or Vaneigem's: 'I love my love so much I wish to give her the magnificent bed of a revolution'. (My own somewhat Eng Lit biased King Lear reference was: 'Love comes empty handed like Cordelia bringing nothing' and that had been culled from Norman O' Brown's book, *Love's Body*).

All old, pre-'68 relationships abandoned, a little later Guy was to take up - and marry - a much younger woman, Alice Becker-Ho which came about most likely as by-product of his growing fame which was reaching the point of adulation. Such meaningless worship possibly contributed to Debord's suicide simply because his razor sharp perceptions couldn't live with the *falsity* of such fame.

Later Bernstein was to marry Ralph Rumney and for a time Ralph lived with her in Salisbury in Wiltshire. Seeing nostalgia was really the only basis between Rumney and Michele it couldn't last and the relationship broke up. Ralph Rumney having broken up with Ms Bernstein, went to live in Monasque, a thoroughly bourgeois town in Haute Provence where he continued to paint and continued to drink himself silly (not that there's anything wrong in the latter activity). He died aged 67 in 2002.

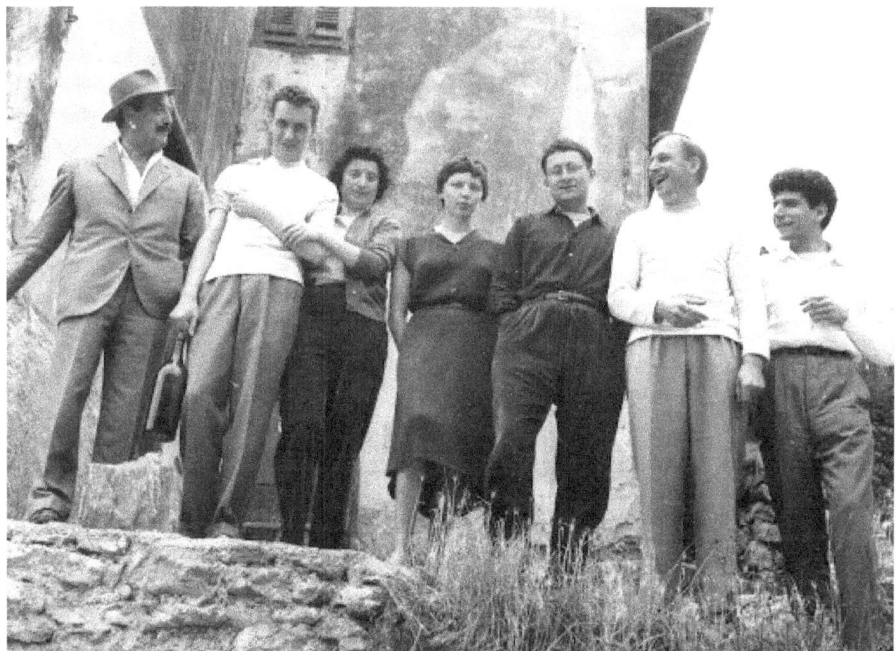

Situationist International founding conference 1967 (Rumney took the photo)

www.ingramcontent.com/pod-product-compliance
Lightning Source LLC
Chambersburg PA
CBHW050100230526
45470CB00004B/1620